ANGKOR & BAYON

UNVEILING THE MEANING AND MYSTERIES

GAVIN P. FRASER

These two temples are like two sides of the same human heart.

Angkor shows the side that respects tradition, ambition, and orderliness.

Bayon shows the side that loves life, fairness, and compassion.

Both are part of who we are.

ISBN 978-1-0369-6310-1

First edition

Development editor: Tim Hammerton

Content editor: Daniel Fraser

Cover Design: Sila Eser, IGUADS. (www.igu.com.tr)

Publisher: Amazon KDP

Typesetting and layout: Andy Thesen DTP

All photographs by author

For Tristan, Lily and Daniel

PREFACE

Most visitors leave Angkor Wat and Bayon amazed—
often overheated and perhaps a little confused. This
book is here to fix that—to make your visit fun, clear,
and maybe even a little profound. It's not about how
high the towers are, but what these buildings say
about two very different ways of seeing the world.

Every year millions of travellers come to Siem
Reap. Many rise before dawn and rush to get in place
to view the first glow of sunlight over the towers
of **Angkor** (**Angkor Wat**). For a few minutes, the air
is magic. After sunrise the guides begin their tours
giving dates, dimensions and dynasties. Tourists nod
politely, but by mid-morning many are already tired,
overwhelmed and a little bored. "The hotel swimming
pool bar is calling me" I heard someone say.

This book is the cure for that feeling. It shows why
Angkor and Bayon are not "just more stones" but
two very different voices proclaiming in stone. Both
were built during the golden age of the **Khmer Empire**
about **800 years ago**: Angkor was largely complete
in 1150 CE and Bayon in 1218 CE. But one speaks of
order, power, and royal control. The other speaks of
compassion, faces, and the life of ordinary people.
Together, they are not relics of the past, but a mirror

FIGURE 1: Angkor Wat West façade

of choices we all face—whether to live by rules and tradition or by care and community, or both.

If **Angkor** is like **Gustave Eiffel's perfect tower**—overwhelming, all order and balance, reaching straight up to heaven—**Bayon** is **Jørn Utzon's Sydney Opera House**: stylish, playful, confusing to navigate, but full of movement and life in every direction.

I have been to Cambodia six times, and I'm still not done. If you've been once, returning is even better. I love the country and especially Siem Reap—the food, the people, the temples, the circus, the museum, the shops, the nightlife and even the traffic. Honestly, I could live the rest of my life there quite happily—provided someone else drives the *remorque*.

A *remorque* (French for trailer) in **Siem Reap** is Cambodia's answer to the limousine—if the limousine had open sides and an engine that sounds like it's

FIGURE 2: Author at Bayon South façade

clearing its throat. It's basically a motorbike pulling a tiny chariot, and somehow it works perfectly.

You climb in, hold on, and instantly feel like royalty on a budget—hair flying, dust swirling, the driver weaving through traffic with Zen-like calm. There are no seatbelts, no doors, and absolutely no chance of pretending you're not a tourist. You can take a car, or cycle if you can stand the heat and distance. For me, there's also no better way to see the temples: the smells of lemongrass and petrol, the smiles of kids shouting "hello!", and the feeling that you are part of the world's friendliest rollercoaster.

The first time I visited, I did what every polite tourist does: I hired a guide. He was excellent—cheerful, well-rehearsed, and armed with an encyclopaedia of dates, dimensions, and dynasties. The second time, I hired another guide, just in case the first had missed something. He hadn't. But, by the third temple, my brain had quietly gone into power-saving mode.

To keep my brain awake I began asking awkward questions. "Why are the most sacred and central parts of Angkor undecorated while the distant corners are meticulously carved?" "What on earth are those buildings called 'libraries', open to the rain and apparently designed for soaking books?" And "who really are those faces on the towers of the Bayon temple?" The answers only produced more questions—and occasionally a polite smile from the guide that said, "that's what the archaeologists have told us".

I strongly recommend hiring a guide—it makes a big difference. But reading this book *before* you go, or even afterwards, will help you enjoy the temples much more and see them with new eyes.

I learned that only 0.1% of Cambodians today are Hindu, which partly explains why Hinduism's deep symbolism in Angkor can seem mysterious. But the architecture is unmistakably Hindu—even if, over time, Buddhism moved in and redecorated, much as the Hagia Sophia in Istanbul changed from cathedral to mosque. The architecture of Angkor breaks all the moulds and traditions—but why?

The Bayon Temple (originally called the Victory Mountain) was no less puzzling. The many guides I have hired and talked to don't confidently explain this very Mahayana or Vajrayana Buddhist architecture—a radically different branch of Buddhism to that practiced in Cambodia these days. And they disagree about whose faces smiled from those towers—gods, kings, or some divine mash-up. It became my personal mystery to solve.

So, I did what any curious (and slightly obsessed) person would do: I spent months in India, visiting over

200 important temples from north to south, Hindu, Jain, Sikh and Buddhist alike. Then I visited the ancient capitals of Sukhothai and Ayutthaya in Thailand, the temples in Luan Prabang in Laos, and ruined Hindu and working Buddhist temples in Vietnam. I spent time visiting the many Hindu temples around Yogyakarta, Java in Indonesia, including the famous Buddhist mountain-shaped temple, Borobudur, and the Hindu Prambanan temples. Angkor and Bayon are like a dramatic echo of these two remarkable temples built roughly 300 years before. I even visited the Buddha's birthplace and the ruins of his father's palace in Lumbini, Nepal.

I would return periodically to Angkor, trying to fit the puzzle pieces together. No king says, "Let's ignore tradition and build something weird—I'm bored." Big temples mean big reasons. Eventually, the picture became clear—and this book is the result.

Appendix A, titled *A Short (and Sometimes Chaotic) History of Mainland Southeast Asia, 0–1250 CE*, tells the story leading up to the completion of Angkor Wat and the Bayon. You might want to dip into it first for a bit of background. Appendix B picks up the thread from 1250 CE to modern times.

When the French "discovered" Angkor in the mid-19th century, it wasn't really a lost world as they had romantically imagined—the Khmer villagers had been living beside the ruins all along, offering incense and prayers to the ancient stones while the West debated whether they'd found the "Asian Atlantis".

The first European to record Angkor was Henri Mouhot, a French naturalist who visited in 1860. He was amazed, scribbling in his diary that these temples rivalled "the greatest monuments of Greece and Rome". (He also assumed the Khmer people couldn't possibly have built them—a mistake that still makes historians roll their eyes.) Mouhot died soon after, bitten by a mosquito in Laos, but his travel journals, published posthumously in 1863, inspired a wave of curiosity that helped France justify its new protectorate over Cambodia, signed that same year. The logic was simple: if you can't own the past, at least own the country it's in.

Étienne Aymonier mapped the temples in the 1870s and 1880s, leaving detailed (and occasionally wild) guesses which trickle down to this day.

Louis Delaporte shipped statues and fragments back to France—where Paris still enjoys them at the Musée Guimet.

Henri Parmentier, George Groslier, and later Maurice Glaize and Jean Commaille led major clearing and restoration works from 1908 through the 1930s.

After World War II, the meticulous Bernard-Philippe Groslier (son of George) brought modern archaeological methods—and a dash of existential philosophy—to the site. He saw temples as mirrors of the human condition—pride, hope, suffering, and belief carved into rock. He asked "Why did people build this? What were they trying to say about life and death?" rather than only "When was it built and by whom?" He believed that understanding Angkor was also about understanding what it means to be human, to create beauty in the face of time and decay.

These archaeologists gave the world what we now call "Angkor", "Bayon", and "the Terrace of the Elephants", but also left a trail of creative mislabelling: "libraries" with no books, "unfinished galleries" that were actually complete, and the occasional "palace" that may have been a pantry.

To the Khmer people, the French were both a curiosity and a disruption. Locals helped as guides and labourers, tolerated the foreigners' hats and measuring rods, and quietly smiled at their certainty. For the Khmer, these were living temples, not "discoveries". The French, however, treated them like sleeping beauty castles, waiting for a kiss from civilisation.

By the time Cambodia regained independence in 1953, the French had cleared thousands of tonnes of jungle and catalogued miles of carvings—though not always correctly. Since then, international teams from Japan, India, Italy, Germany, and the United States have joined the restoration, often undoing or re-doing the French efforts with more respect for the original Khmer engineering.

Today, thanks to over a century of careful (and sometimes comical) archaeology, restoration continues at Angkor and Bayon. They are revered again—part Khmer soul, part international passion project, and proof that even in archaeology, assumptions take longer to remove than jungle vines.

Meanwhile, as I was touring temples in all parts of Asia, the modern world was having its own battles— not in stone, but at the ballot box. The growing political wars between "left" and "right", conservatives and progressives, made me realise something surprising: Angkor and Bayon are not just architectural contrasts—they are two worldviews carved in stone that correspond closely to the rifts in society today. One stands for order and tradition; the other for compassion, caring and community. Built just sixty years apart, they mirror the same human tensions that fill today's headlines.

This book is my attempt to solve the temple mysteries and to share how they represent two opposite world-views—without sending you to sleep in the process. It's short, light-hearted, and full of corny humour to keep even the weary sunrise tourist awake until lunchtime.

In this book I am asking what these temples say about their builder's vision of how a nation should live and be led—and how that vision affected millions of lives.

All around the world, people were also building and searching for meaning in stone, story, and ritual. In Europe, cathedrals like Notre Dame in Paris and Chartres were rising with tall towers and coloured glass. In Africa, the first great stone walls of Zimbabwe were being built. In Asia, the Song dynasty in China built the 2-kilometre-long Anping Bridge in Fujian. In India, temples at Thanjavur and Khajuraho glowed with carvings of gods and dancers. Across the oceans, the Maya city of Chichén Itzá was crowded with pyramids and markets, while in Peru the Chimú began Chan Chan, the largest mud-brick city in the world.

Angkor and Bayon were part of this same global wave of sacred building. What Europe, Africa, Asia, and the Americas were doing in wood, brick, or stone, the Khmer were doing too—but on a scale that still makes jaws drop today.

If you find yourself laughing, learning, or simply nodding as you wipe the sweat from your brow—then, like me, you'll feel it too: at Angkor and Bayon, the stones are not just old, they are alive, whispering across the centuries to tell us about the choices we have today, and how little we have really changed.

Part I of this book tells the story of two very different kings—and their two very different religions. It also gives an easy overview of the design of the temples and how they were built, the kind of sculpture you see everywhere, some clever answers to the great temple mysteries, and a glimpse of what life was like for everyday people at the time.

Part II dives in a bit deeper. It's **a step-by-step guide for visiting each temple**, showing you where to walk, what to look at, and how to understand the long story friezes carved into the walls.

Some readers may prefer to enjoy **Part I** *before visiting the temples*, or on the flight to Cambodia, and then hire a local guide for the sightseeing. Others may want to keep this book in hand when they visit the temples—it talks less like a guidebook and more like a cheerful friend who actually knows what's going on and where to look. Either way, you'll get a humorous and easy-to-follow view of these astonishing temples.

Contents

List of Figures

PART I

CHAPTER 1

TWO KINGS, TWO RELIGIONS

King Suryavarman II

Suryavarman II ruled in the early 1100s. His name
means "Protected by the Sun", and he built **Angkor**, the
largest religious monument in the world. He was **Hindu**
and chose **Vishnu**, the god of order and preservation, as
his divine partner. His temple reflects that choice: strict
lines, perfect symmetry, towers pointing to the sky.
   Suryavarman was like a master engineer or a CEO.
He wanted law, order, and respect, and he carved them
in stone. If you want a Western comparison, he was
a little like **Charlemagne**, the emperor who brought
unity and law to medieval Europe. Angkor is his
legacy—a monument as precise as anything Gustave
Eiffel ever built, but eight centuries earlier and in
sandstone, not iron.

Hinduism in the Khmer Empire

When **Suryavarman II** built Angkor, Hinduism was the
main religion of the **Khmer elite**. This religion began
in India more than 3,000 years ago and has no single

founder. Over time, it grew from ancient books of songs and rituals into a religion that teaches people to live with good behaviour (*dharma*), to understand that every action has results (*karma*), and to aim for freedom from the cycle of rebirth (*moksha*). At its heart were three gods:

- **Brahma**, the creator, with four heads looking in all directions.
- **Vishnu**, the preserver, who kept order in the universe.
- **Shiva,** the destroyer and renewer, who ended things so new life could begin.

Hinduism came to the Khmer kingdom (in today's Cambodia) through Indian traders, travellers, and teachers starting around the 1st century CE. The Khmer kings learned from Indian ideas about kingship, art, and temples.

Angkor was dedicated to **Vishnu**, the god of order. Its perfect symmetry reflects the ideas of order and stability and its long causeways and west-facing design reflect eternity. The temple itself is like a giant symbol of the cosmos, with its moat representing the cosmic ocean and its five towers representing the mythical **Mount Meru,** home of the gods—the Hindu Mount Olympus.

Think of Hinduism in the Khmer Empire as the religion of kingship and tradition. It gave rulers like **Suryavarman II** the divine support to rule with authority, and it gave Angkor its solemn power. In the same way Christianity shaped the Gothic cathedrals of Europe, Hinduism shaped Angkor—with stories from the *Mahabharata* and *Ramayana*, Hindu's epic stories, illuminating many of its key moral principles on Angkor and Bayon's walls.

The *Mahabharata*, written between 400 BCE and 400 CE is India's ultimate family soap opera—a giant story about cousins who can't share a kingdom, full of gods, heroes, flying arrows, and moral lectures. It's as if *Game of Thrones* had a guru who stopped every battle to explain karma and good behaviour.

The *Ramayana*, composed a little earlier, around 500–100 BCE, by the poet Valmiki, is the greatest heroic rescue adventure of Asia—**Prince Rama** loses his wife **Sita** to a demon king who abducts her, builds a bridge with monkey engineers, and marches across the sea to rescue her. Think Liam Neeson in *Taken* where Rama has a "special set of skills" with a bow and arrow.

These two Sanskrit epics were as well-known to the Khmer as the Bible was in medieval Europe or **Homer's** *Iliad* and *Odyssey* were in Greece. That's why the walls of Angkor and Bayon are alive with their scenes—chariots, flying demons, monkey armies, and moral victories—the blockbuster cinema of the ancient world, carved forever in stone.

King Jayavarman VII

Jayavarman VII came to power in 1181, following four short-reigned successors of Suryavarman II. He built **Bayon** after defeating the **Cham** in a major attack on the Khmer Empire. The Cham are a people from central and southern **Vietnam** who long ago built the kingdom of **Champa**, a rich culture influenced by India, with many beautiful Hindu and Buddhist temples. They often attacked the Khmer kingdom because the two neighbours competed for power, land, and control of rich trade routes along the coast.

Jayavarman VII fought back, took the throne, and ruled for nearly 40 years. His name predictably means "Protected by Victory", and his reign really did change the Empire.

Unlike **Suryavarman II**, **Jayavarman VII** followed
Mahayana Buddhism, which taught compassion
and care for all beings. Although he was successful
militarily, he was apparently affected by the slaughter
of war. He searched for answers to the moral cost of
victory and the suffering it left in its wake. His first
wife, **Jayarajadevi**, was a devout and highly informed
Buddhist teacher and poet and influenced him
strongly. She tragically died young, and **Jayavarman**
married her sister, **Indradevi**, who continued in her
footsteps.

Mahayana Buddhism started in India about 2,000
years ago, a few hundred years after the Buddha we all
know lived. As a more elaborate version of Buddhism, it
taught that everyone could reach enlightenment in *one
lifetime*, and that the greatest goal that one could have
is to help all living beings find peace and freedom from
suffering as soon as possible. The way of achieving
this peace is through the help of a divine being (like
a personal coach) called a **Bodhisattva**. These are kind
and wise beings who delay their own nirvana to come
back and help others. The most famous Bodhisattva is
Avalokiteshvara.

Buddhism grew out of Hinduism. While Buddhism
is a separate religion with its own scriptures and
teachings, it still reflects many of the spiritual ideas
and disciplines that came from ancient Hindu thought.
You can think of them as "sister traditions" that
developed side by side, influencing each other over
many centuries. Both practice **meditation** and **yoga** and
believe in the cycle of **reincarnation**.

Mahayana Buddhism spread from India along
trade routes to **China**, and from there to many parts
of Asia, including the **Khmer** kingdom. It became
strong in Cambodia around the 12th century under

Jayavarman VII. Through the influence of his wives, he built not only temples but also roads and public buildings such as resthouses for travellers, places for teaching Buddhism and 102 hospitals—the first known large scale social infrastructure projects in Southeast Asia. Although the aristocracy were still keen on Hinduism, the shock from the attack by the Cham and the destruction of the palace and towns surrounding Angkor severely damaged the people's confidence that the Hindu gods could protect them. Jayavarman VII may therefore have been motivated by royal legitimacy more than anything else to conveniently switch to Buddhism!

His greatest temple was Bayon, at the centre of his new walled capital city Angkor Thom It's roughly four kilometres from Angkor—a 10-minute breezy *remorque* ride through tall trees and quiet stretches of ancient road, often with monkeys watching from the moat walls and city gates.

Bayon is filled with giant smiling faces that seem to watch from every tower. Some say they are the Bodhisattva Avalokiteshvara (also known as Lokeshvara). Others say they are the king himself. They are probably neither of these. We will solve this mystery shortly. Either way, they give the impression of a ruler who wanted to be seen as a caring presence.

In Western terms, Jayavarman VII is a little like Hadrian, the Roman emperor who built walls, roads, and public works across his empire. Hadrian ruled with a thoughtful heart. He loved Greek ideas and learning about people. He accepted that life includes change, pain, and death, and believed—like the Buddha or Lao Tzu—that real strength comes from kindness, compassion and understanding.

Mahayana Buddhism in the Khmer Empire

The most important Bodhisattva, **Avalokiteshvara**, the figure of compassion, is found in many representations in Asia. In **China** he changed and became Guanyin, often shown as a motherly female figure. In Europe she reminds many of Mary, the mother of Jesus.

Mahayana Buddhism gave **Jayavarman VII** a different way to rule. Instead of showing himself as a god-king, he showed himself as a compassionate king.

If Hinduism gave **Angkor** its law and order, Mahayana Buddhism gave **Bayon** its warmth and humanity. One is about reinforcing religious hierarchy, rules and tradition. The other is about caring and helping people as life unfolds.

Both kings wanted heaven on earth—but one built it with overwhelming splendour, the other with care. You can see their beliefs not in their words, but in their walls—Angkor Wat marches in straight lines, Bayon dances in circles.

CHAPTER 2

TWO UNIQUE AND DIFFERENT DESIGNS

If Angkor represents the centre of the universe, Bayon is the centre of the religious state.

Angkor

People say "big" too easily.
  A burger can be big.
  A traffic jam can be big.
  But Angkor Wat?—Angkor Wat is *another level of big*.
  It covers about 1.6 square kilometres—or about 200 football fields—all wrapped inside a moat almost as wide as the Thames or the Seine, and nearly 6 kilometres long to sail all the way around.
  The **Taj Mahal** could sit comfortably in one corner and still feel shy. **St Peter's Basilica** in Rome— the biggest church in the world—could fit in the courtyard and still be asking for directions to the exit. The **Sagrada Família** in Barcelona would look like a small souvenir version standing next to **Angkor's** five towers. Angkor doesn't just make you feel small ... it makes St Peter's feel small too.

In Indian architecture, temples usually come in two big families:

- Dravidian in the South—large colourful gates, multiple concentric walls and courtyards, one inside another like Russian dolls, each enclosure holier than the previous.
- Nagara in the North—built on a raised platform, with curving, vertical towers that rise like mountain peaks, pillars with intricate relief carvings such as Apsaras.

But somewhere in between, especially in central India (Deccan region), architects got creative and invented a third type around the same time as Angkor was built—the Vesara style, meaning "mixed" or "hybrid". It blended the geometry and enclosure walls of the South with the vertical tower profiles of the North. The Chennakesava Temple in Belur is the prototype Vesara masterpiece—not too North, not too South, just right.

When Suryavarman II ordered the development of Angkor, his builders made a Khmer version of Vesara. But if Chennakesava is a violin, Angkor is the whole orchestra in scale and brilliance.

From Southern India's Dravidian style, they took the concentric walls and courtyards. But they left out the tall, fancy gopuras (gateway towers) that usually guard Dravidian temples—perhaps too showy for Khmer taste. They also dropped the open pillared mandapas (halls) typical of Tamil temples like Brihadeeswarar.

From Northern India's Nagara style, they borrowed the idea of rising shikhara-like towers, stacked tiers pointing to heaven, with the god's shrine in the centre—a "mountain for Vishnu". But instead of the usual rounded tower, they sharpened it into a five-pointed lotus—half mountain, half geometry lesson.

The whole complex was aligned and measured like a cosmic diagram, yet uniquely rotated 180 degrees to face west, unlike any Indian model.

The result: a perfect architectural smoothie—half Dravidian discipline, half Nagara grace, blended into a new Khmer Vesara. While India gave Angkor its ingredients, Cambodia made the recipe its own. Angkor is really the "Vesara gone international". But, by facing west, it is unique.

Bayon

If Angkor is a royal symphony, Bayon is jazz. Bayon looks nothing like its tidy neighbour. It has no neat rectangles, and no grand entrance over its own moat that says, "start here".

Instead, towers rise like giant cupcakes with faces—about 200 of them—smiling in every direction as if to say, "Don't worry, enlightenment is everywhere".

When King Jayavarman VII decided to build Bayon, he wanted a new kind of temple—not for a god-king like before, but for a compassionate ruler who smiled back at his people. To do that, he borrowed ideas from everywhere—India, Java, and his own Khmer backyard—then mixed them into something completely new.

Bayon's spirit comes mainly from Mahayana Buddhism. The design is based on a step pyramid. Temples such as Nalanda Monastery (in Bihar, India, 5th–12th century) inspired Bayon's idea of a spiritual city of towers, each honouring wisdom and compassion rather than power.

The biggest Buddhist visual inspiration may have come from Borobudur in central Java, Indonesia—a giant stone mandala shaped like a mountain. However, Jayavarman VII didn't throw out local Khmer tradition.

He built Bayon in the centre of Angkor Thom, right next to older Hindu "mountain temples" like Baphuon and Phimeanakas, built 150 to 200 years before, which are even closer in design to Bayon than Borobudur.

In fact, Bayon has a slightly more elaborate entrance in the east than from any of the other compass directions. This is not normal for Mahayana Buddhist temples. They usually follow Feng Shui principles and face south. Hindu temples traditionally face east. Like many aspects with Bayon, *it brings together both Hindu and Buddhist symbols*, much like Jayavarman and his wives.

The design of Bayon is a bit of a trickster. If you draw a line from east to west, everything is symmetrical. But when you turn and look north to south, it suddenly feels like a different architect took over after lunch and forgot to check the plan. Angkor Wat does the same thing, though with a little more discipline; Bayon, on the other hand, seems to enjoy being unpredictable.

Some archaeologists say its design follows a Vajrayana Buddhist mandala (the third major branch of Buddhism known as Tibetan Buddhism), and that the very name "Bayon" comes from someone mixing up the word Vajrayana—a kind of ancient game of broken telephone. The funny thing is that all true Vajrayana and Mahayana mandalas are *perfectly symmetrical*. If Bayon really was built on that principle, the builders must have been feeling unusually creative … or simply ran out of measuring tape. For me, there is no truth in the Vajrayana Buddhism link to Bayon, least of all its design.

Outside the Temple Walls—Fields and Terraces

When we think of temples, we often focus on walls, towers and carvings. But the spaces outside the walls were just as important—places for parades, festivals, and public display. And here too, Angkor and Bayon differ.

At Angkor, the temple sits inside a huge outer enclosure with a moat. Within this perimeter are wide open fields, perfect for royal processions, elephant parades, and military shows. Imagine over 600,000 to 1.2 million people standing in the inner fields, and also on either side of the moat, watching as the king rode past high on an elephant, banners flying, and music playing. The outer grounds were the stage for power— large, ordered, and built to impress. It was the Khmer Empire's stadium and a refuge in times of war, similar to the southern temple style in India.

At Bayon, things are different. Bayon itself has no great enclosure of its own—only the distant narrow moat and city walls of Angkor Thom. It is rather like a grand traffic circle with roads leading out in the four points of the compass. In this way it is more like Notre Dame in Paris, St Paul's in London, Cologne Cathedral and the Duomo in Florence. That means its temple grounds were tighter, more crowded. When Jayavarman VII wanted parades and displays, he built the Elephant Terrace (named after the carvings on the wall) just down the road. The king and nobles sat above the crowds on a raised platform, while below in the open ground, dancers, musicians and troops with elephants performed.

While Angkor kept its parades inside its own moat and walls, Bayon's civic life spilled into the city itself. Angkor was self-contained, like a private palace with its own stadium. Bayon was built into the main thoroughfare of the capital—more like a city square, open to everyone.

CHAPTER 3

SAME BUILDING PROCESS, TWO DIFFERENT SPEEDS

Different dreams, yes—but both kings used the same earth, same stone, and very tired builders. Both Angkor and Bayon were huge projects. They were made by armies of workers, stonecutters, and carvers—whole cities of people organised around a king's vision.

Angkor

Building Angkor took around 35 years. It was all built by hand, in the 12th century, with stone blocks weighing up to 1,500 kilograms each. No cranes, no trucks, no concrete—just human muscle, bamboo and elephants.

Angkor was planned with military precision. The site was levelled and drained, so the ground stayed firm even during monsoon rains. Its perfect symmetry was achieved by careful measurement with ropes, bamboo grids, and alignment with the sun and stars.

The huge surrounding rectangular moat, symbolising the cosmic ocean, helped control flooding and supplied

FIGURE 3: Angkor's moat—the cosmic ocean

water for construction. The moat was necessary to keep the soil under Angkor moist: if it dried out and shrank, the weight of the building above could cause it to lean and topple over.

The temple used about 5 million tons of stone. After a layer of sand, builders used laterite for the inside (the cake) and sandstone for the outside (the icing). Laterite is a reddish, iron-rich stone common in Cambodia. It is light when freshly cut but hardens when exposed to air, making it ideal for foundations and inner walls. It is volcanic, like the pumice stone popular with people who use it to soften the skin on their feet.

Laterite is visible in the outer walls and steps near the moat: look closely at the base of the outer enclosure walls or under stairways—you'll see rough, reddish-brown blocks full of small holes, like an old sponge.

Sandstone produces a finer finish when carved and honed. If you go further, it polishes to a shine, as you

FIGURE 4: Laterite blocks topped by sandstone layer: Lions and Naga halfway along the walkway across Angkor's moat

see on some of the sculptures. Sandstone blocks were cut from quarries at Mount Kulen, 50 kilometres away. They were floated down rivers and canals on rafts, then dragged into place on rollers by men and elephants and put in place without mortar. This means they would better stand the test of time since mortar can weather and flake away just like the grouting of the tiles in your bathroom. The walls line up so cleanly that engineers today still admire the precision.

The corridor roofs use corbelled arches—each stone overlapping the one below it, form both sides, until a few layers later they meet in the middle, like layers of Lego.

Wood played a big part, not only during construction, but in the decorative finishing of the building. The outer galleries had carved wooden ceilings—some have been reinstalled in Angkor to show how they would have appeared. Painted panels were fixed into stone slots still visible on bare walls today.

Bright pigments (red, green, gold) decorated door frames and reliefs—a far cry from the grey we see now. We'll talk more about it later—when we try to solve the great mystery of "Unfinished Angkor".

One of the crowning glories of Angkor is its sculpted surfaces. These aren't just building stones; they are works of art. We will explore these further on.

Bayon

Bayon, built about 60 years later, took maybe 20–25 years to complete. The design seems to have developed as work progressed. It appears as if Jayavarman was keen to get it built as quickly as possible, as it was intended for his life, not his death. Corridors twist, towers crowd together and inner temples in the four corners of Level 2 appear different. Stones sometimes do not quite meet giving the impression that stairs were built simultaneously by different teams who had a rough plan but who were working from different ends trying to meet in the middle. To modern eyes it feels messy and complicated, but it also feels human.

As Bayon stands in the middle of Angkor Thom, the king's walled city which has its own moat, there is no dedicated temple moat here. There are pools either side of the four main entrances that represent the cosmic ocean.

Bayon used less stone than Angkor—around 1 million tons of laterite in the body and another million of sandstone externally—but it's packed into a smaller space like an overfilled lunch box. Each tower had a stone roof, made from corbelled arches (stones stacked in curves, no keystones or cement).

The carvings at Bayon are different from Angkor's neat, formal style. They look more alive, sometimes uneven, sometimes crowded—but full of movement.

That's because many were cut directly onto the stone *before* the stones were put in place, and by teams working fast.

Angkor is the meticulously detailed blueprint; Bayon is the committee brainstorm. And yet both still stand.

When the basic structure was completed, the decoration began—gods, dancers, monsters, and guardians stepped out of the rock.

CHAPTER 4

DEVATAS, APSARAS, NAGAS, AND LIONS

Khmer Style

The sculpture at Angkor and Bayon are not about muscles or perfect geometry. At Angkor, bodies twist gracefully in every direction—smooth and idealised, rather than veiny or muscular, yet bursting with strength and energy.

At Bayon, the figures are chunkier and gentler— less about muscle, more about softness and flow, often caught in quiet moments of daily tasks and meditation. Bodies are round, not rigid or tense. Faces are serene, eyes half closed, lips almost smiling—like someone who knows the secret to peace *and* good posture.

Compare that with the Greek classical style, like on the **Parthenon** frieze: there, everybody is lean, athletic, and caught mid-action—runners, riders, gods with six-packs. It's all about movement, control, and ideal proportion. **Greek** art says, "Look how perfect the human form can be." **Khmer** art says, "Look how peaceful the human spirit can be." One celebrates energy and anatomy; the other celebrates harmony and eternity.

For readers familiar with the world of sculpture, Khmer sculpture has its echoes in **Auguste Rodin** (1840–1917), **Henry Moore** (1898–1986) and **Fernando Botero** (1932–2023): the humorous one sculpting the larger figure.

Rodin's famous sculpture, *The Kiss*, has the same soft, rounded energy. Muscles are there, but they *breathe*; emotion lives under the skin. Rodin admired Asian art deeply, especially for its sense of stillness and inner life.

Moore's reclining figures—big, curvy, and abstract— feel like modern cousins of Bayon's people. They share the same organic rhythm and sense that the human form belongs to nature, not just to art.

Fernando Botero's figures are famously plump, but full of joy and balance—like Apsaras (see below) who discovered ice cream. His art, like Bayon's, celebrates roundness as a kind of generosity.

We will get to the famous carved walls (friezes) shortly. But first we should describe the other decorative carving and free-standing sculpture you will see everywhere at Angkor and Bayon, common in Hindu temples all over the world, though at Bayon, it takes a Buddhist twist.

Devata—Divine beings or goddesses

Devatas and **Apsaras** (described in the next section) are found at both Angkor and Bayon. What you will see is that Devatas are everywhere at Angkor, and Apsaras dominate Bayon. They are two different kinds of heavenly beings.

Devatas are the temple's security guards—keeping watch in key positions, standing still, or posing slightly, serious, and behaving. They are carved to guard the temple and watch those moving around.

In Hindu and Buddhist belief, Devatas are minor deities or divine attendants, born from the cosmic imagination of the gods to help protect the universe. They appear in many roles—guardians of directions, rivers, trees, or temples.

When the **Khmer** sculptors filled **Angkor**'s walls with Devatas, they turned these heavenly helpers into graceful stone women, each wearing jewellery, high crowns, and calm expressions. They weren't meant to dance—they were meant to watch, bless, and keep the peace.

FIGURE 5: Angkor Devatas

FIGURE 6: Bayon Devatas

FIGURE 7: Angkor Apsaras

Apsaras—Celestial nymph, dancer, or water spirit

If temples had stars, the Apsaras would be them. They appear in almost every Hindu temple from India to Cambodia, showing the joy and grace of heaven. In India, they usually float high on the walls or ceilings, dancing for the gods, never for ordinary people.

Apsaras are carved to show movement, to make the walls come alive. Devatas keeps heaven in order—Apsaras keep heaven entertained.

At **Angkor**, the Apsaras keep their distance. You'll find them up in the air, gliding in perfect formation like a flock of birds in paradise. In the great frieze of the *Churning of the Ocean of Milk* (detailed in Part II), they hover above the chaos, watching gods and demons tug their giant serpent below. They are not individuals. They are carved in a repeated pattern, each evenly spaced from the other.

FIGURE 8: Bayon Apsaras

They also appear again high on the lintels above pillars in the criss-crossing colonnades around the lower four sacred pools at Angkor, just under the curved ceilings—always elegant, always out of reach, barely seen. They also appear at the highest points of Angkor, on the central Mount Meru. They dance for heaven, not for us.

At **Bayon**, everything changes. The Apsaras have come down to earth. You'll meet them at eye level as you arrive at Bayon, individually, in groups of two or three. They are carved on the outer pillars of the temple opposite the lower frieze (explained in Part II). They're much larger, livelier, and completely individual—no two faces or poses are the same. They are dancing rather than flying. One foot is in the air and one on a lotus, as if auditioning singly or in pairs or trios of friends for "Bayon's got Talent". They have come down from heaven to meet you and welcome you. They twist, smile, and dance as if to say, "Blessings on you. The gods can wait; this one's for the people."

While **Angkor's** Apsaras seem far away and float in perfect order, **Bayon's** Apsaras dance in glorious freedom—just like the temples themselves.

Nagas—Serpent or Cobra

Thirdly, every bridge and walkway usually ends at a Naga. Nagas are sacred serpent beings from Hindu and Buddhist mythology, and at Angkor and Bayon they appear everywhere—guarding bridges, gates, and stairways with their many heads spread like fans. Often within the fan the figure of a god emerges, most often **Vishnu**.

In legend, the Naga was the ancestor of the **Khmer** people, born from the marriage of an Indian prince and a Naga princess—so in Cambodia, the Naga isn't just decoration, it's family.

Symbolically, Nagas are protectors of water and life, keeping the balance between the heavens and the underworld. Their stone bodies stretch like living bridges between worlds—a reminder that when you walk beside one at Angkor and Bayon, you're moving from earthly life to the realm of the gods.

FIGURE 9: Naga at Angkor

Incidentally, entering the city of Angkor Thom from whatever corner of the compass, you cross a stone bridge over the moat. There is a giant snake on either side, but this is not a Naga but a very particular creature. This is Vasuki, the serpent who the gods and monsters were using to stimulate the production of all good things in the universe, in particular amrita, the nectar of immortality. This story is repeated several times at Angkor and at Bayon and is known as "The Churning of the Ocean of Milk". Although Vasuki appears on both sides of bridges, you are seeing the two ends of the same snake.

Lions

You'll meet lions all around Angkor and Bayon—though none of them ever roared. These stone guardians stand proudly at stairways and gateways, their job is to protect the temple from evil spirits and to show royal power. In Hindu and Buddhist art, the lion (called *simha* in Sanskrit) is the symbol of strength, courage, and the voice of truth—the roar of the Buddha's teaching.

FIGURE 10: Angkor Lions

FIGURE 11: Bayon Lion and Naga

At **Angkor**, the lions are elegant and disciplined, like palace guards on parade. Their bodies are sleek, their faces calm, their manes carved in neat curls—perfectly in step with **Suryavarman II**'s taste for symmetry and control. They match the temple's grand, orderly spirit: all about perfection and authority.

At **Bayon**, the lions look a little different. They are chunkier, rougher, and sometimes slightly off-balance, as if they might jump down and join the crowd in the carvings. Their smiles (yes, even lions here smile) fit **Jayavarman VII**'s warmer, more human world— protective but friendly, strong but approachable.

The difference tells a story: Angkor's lions guard a king's heaven; Bayon's guard a people's city. One watches in silence; the other seems ready to laugh with you.

CHAPTER 5

THE MYSTERIES SOLVED

MYSTERY One: The "Libraries"—What Were They Really For?

Walk through Angkor or Bayon, and you'll spot a few small stone buildings sitting politely off to the side—like they're waiting for someone to remember

FIGURE 12: Angkor "library", Level 1

what they were built for. At Angkor, there are two on the long walk before you reach the raised causeway into the temple proper, two more in the lower grassy courtyard on Level 2, and another pair up in the upper paved courtyard at Level 4. Bayon, not wanting to be left out, has its own two "mystery boxes" in the first courtyard on if you enter from the East.

Guides call them "libraries". That idea came from the early French archaeologists, who'd just dusted themselves off from digs in Egypt where they did find papyrus scrolls in old rooms. When they arrived in Cambodia and found similar-looking little chambers, they slapped on the same label. It sounded scholarly, and like most good mistakes, it stuck.

But pause for a moment and picture it: open-air rooms with people coming in and out, in a tropical monsoon climate, and with rain falling sideways for half the year—is this the best place to keep delicate palm-leaf manuscripts safe? That's like keeping your diary collection in your shower.

Real temple libraries in the Khmer world were nothing like this. They were small, solid, and sensible—built with thick walls and only narrow doors or slots for light and air, often covered with stone bars. Their job was to protect sacred palm-leaf texts from humidity, insects, and the occasional typhoon, not to invite them in. Think of them as ancient safes rather than reading rooms. The idea that Angkor's open pavilions were ever used to store books is charming—and completely impossible.

Some scholars have also called these little buildings "dancing halls". Now, that's a lovely thought—until you remember what real Indian dancing halls look like. In India, they're grand pillared pavilions, big enough for hundreds of dancers to swirl about while hundreds

FIGURE 13: Angkor "library", Level 2

more watch in admiration. The "libraries" at **Angkor**, by contrast, are about the size of a modern living room. You could maybe squeeze in four dancers if everyone held their breath and agreed not to spin. The idea of a royal performance in one of these would be like trying to stage *Swan Lake* in the garden shed—interesting idea, ridiculous in practice.

Let us start with the first of **Angkor**'s so-called libraries along the entrance causeway: in most Hindu temple complexes, such side buildings outside the main temple were resthouses. Worshippers could sit out a sudden downpour, share a meal, or leave an offering if they weren't properly dressed to enter the main temple. Traditionally men use one side, women the other. Archaeologists found the base of a larger nearby building that was likely a changing hall for those preparing to enter the temple—essentially an ancient locker room for pilgrims. These "libraries" were multi-purpose buildings, not literary lounges. On festival days, they might even have held palanquins for carrying the gods during parades. They were accessible to ordinary people for their use, too far from the main temple for the priests.

Higher up, at Level 2 of Angkor, the "libraries" inside the temple were more like break rooms for the Brahmins—places for priests to rest, eat, wash, and change after performing rituals. Several priests would have attended to each statue, washing and dressing it, accepting offerings of food and incense, and blessing worshippers with paste on their foreheads or sprinkling holy water—as is still done in Hindu temples today. After their shift on the upper terraces, they'd come down to these side rooms to clean up and recharge before the next round of divine duty. The "libraries" at Bayon were more than likely used in this way.

And what about the little stone buildings at Level 4? They were not for eating and changing. That would have been unthinkable. These sit in the realm of the gods beside the King's own processional entrance up Mount Meru, the sacred heart of the temple. Imagine putting the royal penthouse next to the staff canteen—even the gods would frown.

These upper pair of "libraries" were almost certainly shrines, not storerooms, dedicated to Lakshmi (Vishnu's wife) and Garuda (his mount). Early explorers almost got this right, except they mixed up Lakshmi with Parvati, Shiva's wife. That's like saying Romeo and Cleopatra or that Beyoncé tours with George Clooney—entertaining, but not historically sound. They dropped the idea, although they were probably correct. They just gave the one shrine the wrong name.

The position of these shrines along the king's entrance is too important for them to be multifunctional change rooms and dining rooms for monks. These activities would be taking place lower down at Level 2 and not near the "holiest of holies" and certainly not so close to the king.

So yes, these "libraries" had their purposes and were a hub of activity—rest stops, priest rooms, or companion shrines—all depending on where they stood. But one thing is certain: none of them ever housed books. The only reading that went on inside Angkor's "libraries" was probably someone checking a festival schedule.

MYSTERY Two: Is the Centre of Level 2 at Angkor Unfinished?

The question of whether Angkor was left unfinished is one of those enduring archaeological riddles that sounds more dramatic than it is. Two things can, in fact, be true at once. Some parts of Angkor were added later, but the areas that look plain today were not unfinished—they have simply lost their decorations over time.

There is one spot where the carving stopped midway—one window frame with its borders almost completed and a single unfinished devata. This is on the east side of Level 2. But that's all. You can't even see them from the main corridor because they are on the East façade. It looks like work that would have only taken another day to complete. Perhaps the scaffolding was taken down too early, or blown over in a storm, and it wasn't worth reassembling it for a few more chisel strokes. Hardly the mark of a grand but abandoned project.

The second case scholars point to is of the two later friezes either side the northeast corner—

FIGURE 14: Angkor "undecorated" central point

Vishnu battling the demons and Krishna fighting Banasura—which were added in 1564, 400 years after Suryavarman died. These were not "unfinished" when the temple was built; they were completed additions at a later age. At St Paul's Cathedral in London, a brand-new stained-glass window was unveiled in 2022 to honour Queen Elizabeth II's Platinum Jubilee—the first new window there in more than 100 years. But no-one claimed that St Paul's was unfinished until that point.

One could fairly say that Angkor was *intended* to have a continuous wrap-around frieze, but plans were interrupted by war. After Suryavarman's death in 1150, the empire's attention turned to defence, not decoration. Although construction ended when the king died, the temple's existing main friezes were all completed. If a new king opted to not spend money on the military, it would have been spent instead on his own temples.

The real misunderstanding comes from what people call the "unfinished" parts: the focal point corridor intersections and entrance halls. These look bare today but were, in fact, the most elaborately finished

FIGURE 15: Angkor detailed wood carving

spaces in their time, but just not in stone carving like the friezes.

Traces of pigment, designs lightly incised into the stone, and the sockets where wooden panels once fitted all tell the same story: these were not left rough; they have been stripped bare by time. Even today, carved wooden lintels survive in areas sheltered from the weather, and a reconstructed timber ceiling in one gallery shows how richly the halls were dressed. There was wood everywhere—doors, ceilings, wall panels—all of it long gone. Walls were painted or hung with cloth, and carved lines could have been covered in paint or gold leaf.

Ask yourself: would Suryavarman II, who oversaw the largest religious monument on earth and fussed over every last tower, leave the central crossroads undecorated? It's like claiming the craftsman of a Rolls-Royce forgot to put in the dashboard. The truth is that the finishing touches were made in bright, colourful perishable materials. What the weather did not take

away over centuries, war, looters, and colonial collectors stripped away.

A better explanation is that what we see today in parts is Angkor's skeleton—the underlying framework of a building that once glittered with colour and warmth. Those blank walls were never meant to be blank. They once shone with painted plaster, gold leaf, carved wood, (possibly paint as well) and fabric hangings. South Indian temples at Madurai and Thanjavur still show how this would have looked: blazing with reds, blues, and golds. Angkor was the same.

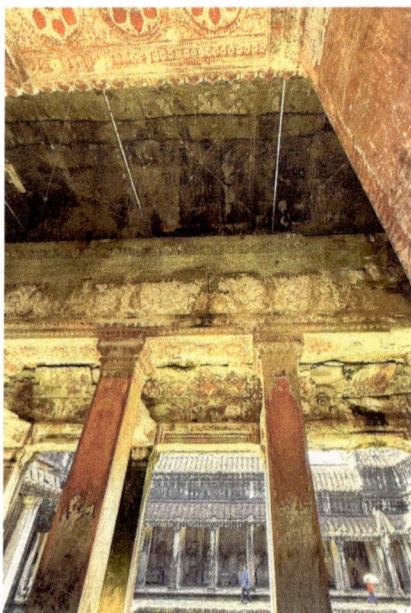

When the Khmer artists began their work, the sandstone was rough, dusty, and rather dull, like bread before it goes into the

FIGURE 16: (top) Angkor carved wooden ceilings, Level 2 corridor

FIGURE 17: (bottom) Angkor Level 3 decoration

oven. To bring life into these walls, they first scratched fine outlines onto the surface: elegant curves, floral borders, the swirl of a crown or the line of a face. These were not meant as decoration themselves to be carved later like a frieze, but as the artist's sketch. They allowed for easy repainting after existing paint wore away. The scratchings would be filled with black paint to outline the figures after the rest of the surface was painted different colours—a real labour saving for

FIGURE 18: Three different Angkor decorations: stone carving, outlined patterns and painted plaster

the artists who did not have to repeatedly paint the outline unsuccessfully with a soft brush, and a way of achieving sharp accurate outlines. Once the designs were in place, the stone was rubbed and polished smooth, ready to receive colour and glory.

Before any paint touched it, the sandstone needed a little help. The artists brushed on a thin layer of gesso—a mixture of lime or fine white clay mixed with sticky resin from trees or boiled animal glue. This acted like a primer, sealing the stone so that colours would stay bright and not disappear into the pores. Think of it as the ancient equivalent of undercoat paint from a hardware shop—necessary, but invisible in the end.

Then came the real fun: the painting. Khmer painters didn't believe in dull gods. They mixed vivid colours from the earth around them—**red ochre** from iron-rich soil, **yellow ochre** from muddy minerals, black from soot or burnt wood, **white** from lime, and when they could find it, **green** or **blue** from crushed **malachite** or **indigo** leaves. These powders were stirred with sticky tree sap, lac resin, or even egg yolk, turning them into a paint that could survive the tropical heat. They then painted the gods and Apsaras—red-skinned, black-haired, with white eyes and warm ochre clothes. The temples must have been full of life and movement, glowing with colour.

For the most sacred figures, paint alone was not enough. They needed the sparkle of heaven itself— gold. To make gold leaf stick, the artists prepared a special layer of fine red or yellow clay mixed with resin or glue. Onto this tacky surface they carefully pressed sheets of gold so thin they could flutter in a breath of air. Then, with a cloth, they burnished it to shine. Crowns, jewels, halos, and even faces gleamed in the

FIGURE 19: Angkor outlines for painters (not unfinished sculpting)

light. Under the Cambodian sun, the temples would have sparkled like palaces of the gods, not grey ruins.

When all the work was done, the result was astonishing. The walls glowed red and yellow; fine black lines outlined each figure so that the carvings seemed almost to move as one walked past. In its full glory, Angkor was no pale temple but a riot of gold, yellow, red, blue, green, and black, shining under the sun and torchlight alike.

When we see the temples today, stripped of colour and worn by rain, we are looking only at the bones of their former splendour. Once, they were as dazzling as any current Thai or Burmese temple—a world of sandstone turned to gold and flame.

To call it "unfinished" is an old French habit, born of seeing ruins through the lens of missing ornament. The truth is more interesting: Angkor is not unfinished—it is unclothed. We are walking through the world's greatest theatre after the stage set and curtain have gone.

If you stand in the centre of Angkor and hear "unfinished", smile politely. Then picture gold, paint, silk, painted wood, and banners. The king would never have left his own mausoleum looking bare.

MYSTERY Three: Who Are the Faces of Bayon?

For centuries, visitors to Bayon have stood beneath those calm, half-smiling faces and wondered: who are they? Gods? Kings? Some mysterious hybrid spirit? The mystery has invited countless theories, but if we apply a little common sense—and a pinch of humour—the suspects quickly begin to eliminate themselves.

We can start with the most obvious candidate: Avalokiteshvara, the Bodhisattva of compassion. He's the favourite explanation in guidebooks and a likely candidate—gentle, kind, the Buddhist equivalent of a celestial social worker.

But look closely. There's no seated Amitabha Buddha in the crown which is a non-starter. This is *the* defining identifier of this Bodhisattva. Amitabha Buddha, known as the Buddha of Infinite Light, is the celestial Buddha who created a pure land of bliss where souls can be reborn through faith and compassion rather than years of meditation. He existed *before* the Buddha we commonly know today.

Also, why would a lower figure in Buddhism be so prominent all over a temple with the actual Buddha hidden away in the central shrine. It is like having dozens of images of John the Baptist in a Church and only one depiction of Jesus Christ. And another thing, the influence of Mahayana Buddhism into the Khmer Empire was from China and Vietnam and Avalokiteshvara had already changed gender to become Guanyin. Some argue that Jayavarman's architects may have looked to a much older form of Mahayana Buddhism, but there is no evidence for this. The Bayon faces are kingly and masculine, not saintly or androgynous. Compassion may be present in the smile, but this is all.

To say that the faces are Avalokiteshvara alone has little to support it, except the smile. It is like saying the Mona Lisa is Guanyin, the female form of Avalokiteshvara. All that can be borrowed from Mahayana Buddhism is the idea of compassion. A religion that cares for you.

Next possible candidates for the faces come the old Hindu heavyweights: Shiva and Vishnu. Grand, powerful, familiar—and entirely impossible. Their must-have symbols are nowhere to be seen: no third eye, no trident, no discus or conch. These were the deities of the past dynasties; the old regime Jayavarman VII was politely retiring. After all, if you are building a new capital after a foreign invasion, and you want to focus on Mahayana Buddhism, you don't advertise yesterday's main gods. Out they go as possibilities.

Perhaps then the Buddha himself (Siddhartha Gautama)? Sensible, serene, respectable—who could object? The problem is that the Buddha isn't a god but an example, an enlightened being who left the world behind. To plaster his face on every tower would be like printing your teacher's photo on every street corner. Besides, his statue already sits in the main shrine, which makes the surrounding stone billboards

FIGURE 20: Bayon's signature faces

redundant. The Buddha keeps his central position, but he doesn't need fifty backup singers.

Then there's the theory that the faces are simply Jayavarman VII himself. The resemblance is tempting— the same broad nose, the same enigmatic smile—but it doesn't quite fit. At any rate, there are thousands of faces that look just like this in the friezes of Angkor and Bayon and they are not Jayavarman VII. They are the ideal of Khmer masculinity. Carving your own face hundreds of times on a Buddhist temple would have looked suspiciously vain. Even for a king, that borders on heresy.

Buddhism prefers humility, not selfies in stone. We must reluctantly dismiss this royal possibility too.

What about Brahma, the Hindu creator god? He, at least, has the right number of faces—four. *It is his defining feature that no other god has.* In later times, the Khmer did add multiple faces, like wedding cakes, to their images of gods and demons, but never just four: these were for Brahma alone looking in the four cardinal directions of the universe, like the four roads radiating out in the cardinal directions from Bayon and over the moat to the ends of the empire.

Brahma is popular in both Hinduism and Buddhism. In modern day Thailand, he is revered as Phra Phrom and his images adorn royal funeral regalia. He is known as the god of wisdom, kindness, building and protection, which were Jayavarman's chief traits, as well as the god of good fortune—not a bad choice. Brahma's wife, Sarasvati, like Jayavarman's own queens, was an educator and patron of learning.

However, as many aristocrats were still Hindu, Jayavarman was too politically smart to alienate them by completely adopting Buddhism. Including the right *senior* Hindu god was a good move, but it could not be Shiva or Vishnu.

In India, Brahma had long since faded from popularity due to a smear campaign involving supposed infidelity and dishonesty; curiously, he got more attention in Angkor than in his homeland. Still, Brahma on his own would have dragged the king back into Vedic tradition, and Jayavarman was busy reinventing the spiritual landscape. He would have to create an image that was Brahma-adjacent, a Buddhist version.

Then there was the architecture. Having all these heads of Brahma with a little crown that had no lotus motif would not work. Buddhist mountain temples had stupas that tapered upwards. Bayon would need these. And lotuses at the top.

This is what I believe Jayavarman and his architects decided: start with the four faced head of Brahma for his Hindu association and popularity with Buddhists, his all-seeing wisdom of a creator, his neutrality, his compassion, his being a builder god and protector with a wife interested in education, spread his face out rather than all faces touching, add a conical tower on top like a stupa, top this with a lotus, and make him look like a Khmer. Brahma always smiles, so if the face was meant to refer to another smiling or compassionate being, all bases were covered.

In the end, the faces of Bayon are not Avalokiteshvara, not Sakyamuni Buddha, not Shiva or Vishnu and not the king alone. They are Brahma in structure topped with Buddhist architecture and capturing the compassionate essence of Mahayana Buddhism. If subjects wanted to see the faces as Jayavarman VII and imagined him as a new Bodhisattva, he may not have objected: the first great monument of compassionate kingship, smiling eternally across the jungle to remind us that power, when softened by mercy, can still look beautiful.

Now that we know a lot more about these two temples, let's imagine what they looked like—not as ruins, but as living, glowing cities of faith.

CHAPTER 6

IMAGINE THE TEMPLES IN THEIR HEYDAY

Close your eyes and forget the jungle for a moment. Picture music, colour, perfume, and a thousand lamps flickering on golden stone.

We walk among ruins today, but 800 years ago, these temples were bursting with colour, sound, and people. Think less "grey ruin" and more "festival ground"— closer to a carnival parade than a museum.

When freshly cut, the Kulen sandstone is a warm golden-beige, sometimes with rosy pink or honey-brown tones. Over time, weather and humidity turned it dull grey—but in its day, it would have glowed in the tropical light, like baked gold at sunrise.

Angkor had golden stone spires rising from green fields and reflecting water. Bayon, would be golden too and alive with colour, perhaps hung with banners and filled with the scent of incense—its smiling towers bright against the jungle backdrop.

At Angkor, under Suryavarman II, the mood was formal. Priests performed rituals, soldiers guarded the king, and elephants processed through the gates.

Nobles and courtiers came to watch or to serve, while artisans carved endless friezes of Hindu epics.

The caste system was clear: Brahmin priests kept the link to the gods; warriors defended the realm; farmers produced rice to feed everyone. Women of high rank sometimes managed estates or religious endowments, while village women spun cloth, wove mats, or carried offerings. Children learned early to work alongside parents. For commoners, life was hard but organised, their role defined in service of a great king and his god **Vishnu**.

At Bayon, under **Jayavarman VII**, the atmosphere shifted. Reliefs show not only battles but also markets, fishing, cooking, and even games. It was as if the temple walls themselves widened to include everyday people. Bayon connected the empire: the constant movement of people and goods for commerce. Buddhism's softer touch—influenced by the king's wives—gave women more visible roles in religion and education. Monks and nuns ran schools and cared for orphans. Farmers still bent over rice fields, and soldiers still fought the **Cham**, but there was also a sense of civic life: hospitals, rest houses, and public works. Children here might grow up seeing their parents not only serve a king but also be part of a community project.

While Angkor tells the story of a god-king and his cosmic order, Bayon shows us a society alive with both palace grandeur and market chatter. One temple was a royal mausoleum, the other almost a living city square.

80 Years Later

The life of the people was recorded by the Chinese scribe **Zhou Daguan** in 1296. By this time, **Jayavarman VII**, the builder of Bayon, had died many years before in 1218. There were three notable kings after him. The first continued his venture into Mahayana Buddhism, the second returned to Hinduism and defaced much of the Buddhist images at Bayon. The third struck an entirely new direction into **Theravada Buddhism**, the version still in Cambodia today.

Jayavarman VII's grand Mahayana vision had filled Cambodia with stone faces, hospitals, and towers—all wonderful, but very costly. The empire couldn't afford such divine architecture anymore. At the same time, the King of **Thailand** in his capital **Sukhothai** had invited monks from **Sri Lanka** and this simpler, cheaper and more personal form of Buddhism captured people's hearts. The focus was on community monks and daily merit-making instead of grand royal monuments. Monks came from Thailand to Cambodia and this religious influence combined with economic and political exhaustion pushed the shift.

Zhou Daguan expected to see a royal palace—but he found much more: a whole world carved from stone, filled with life, noise, and a lot of bare feet.

He wrote that the **Khmer** capital was enormous, bigger than any city in **China** he knew. The king lived in golden splendour. Common people lived in wooden houses raised on stilts, surrounded by palm trees and rice fields. Zhou noticed that everyone bathed often— not for religion, but because it was too hot not to.

The markets amazed him. Women ran everything— buying, selling, gossiping. Men, he said, "do little business", which makes you think the **Khmer** economy ran on female energy. The markets sold fish, fruit, betel nuts, and even crocodile meat—though it is unclear whether Zhou tried it.

He admired the temples, especially **Angkor**, calling it a place of "marvellous work and great labour". But he was less impressed by the mosquitoes and heat. He described monks in saffron robes, families praying, and ordinary people making offerings of flowers and rice.

Zhou noticed strict rules: people took off their shoes before approaching the king, and everyone bowed deeply. Yet life outside the palace was lively—festivals, music, cockfights, and even public wrestling. He laughed at how **Khmer** men wore little more than a cloth wrap, while women's clothes were "light and beautiful".

In short, Zhou Daguan's book *Customs of Cambodia* shows that the Angkor region was not just stone towers and gods—it was a buzzing, happy, sometimes chaotic place full of laughter, trade, devotion, and tropical sweat.

Today the gods may be silent, but the stones still speak—if you know how to listen.

PART II

CHAPTER 7

VISITING THE TEMPLES

Now it's your turn to enter the story—smartphone or camera in one hand, curiosity in the other.

Temples are not just stone. They are also movement—how they guide your feet, your eyes, and even your feelings. Angkor and Bayon push you in very different ways.

At **Angkor**, the plan is clear, straight, and grand. Everything lines up on one axis. The space tells you what to do: walk forward, be quiet, be in awe.

At **Bayon**, the opposite happens. Paths come from every direction, and there are entrance steps everywhere. Inside, the passages twist and confuse. You can easily get lost or turned around, suddenly face-to-face with another visitor or another smiling tower. This is not by accident. Bayon was built as a maze, slowing potential enemies who may attack and forcing people close together. **Jayavarman VII** must have decided that if the **Cham** were to storm and enter Bayon, they would crash into one another in every direction. But it also creates intimacy: you cannot stay distant; you must mix and meet. It feels more like a crowded bazaar or a festival street, alive with surprise.

Angkor's movement is about deference—a king above his people, order above chaos.

Bayon's movement is about closeness—people meeting in corners, a king who walked among his subjects. Both are brilliant, but they lead your body, and your mind, in very different directions.

Start with Angkor

Take about three hours. It is not necessary to arrive to see the sunrise. For many, this is an underwhelming experience. But go after an early breakfast while it is still cool. Take whatever hydration suits you, some little treats and snacks and protection from the sun. Angkor and Bayon both provide shelter, but you will still spend some time walking outside.

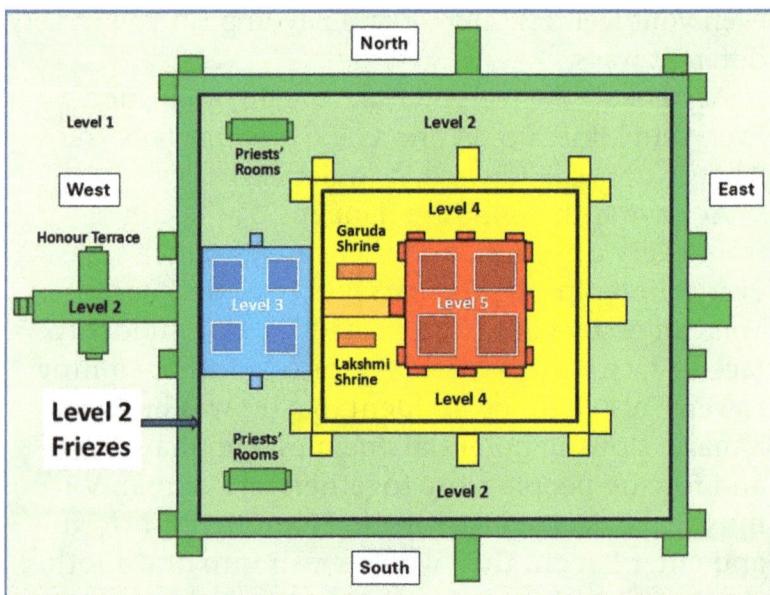

FIGURE 21: Plan view of Angkor Wat

Angkor is a perfectly balanced military parade in stone. The whole of Angkor faces west, which for Hindus is the direction of death—another sign that it was a mausoleum as well as a temple.

You arrive at the western access walkway over the moat. You are met of course by Nagas and lions. The balustrades are Nagas, and proud royal lions guard the entrance. They show readiness and strength, demanding respect as people cross from an earthly shore to a holy island. You will see many of them along the way before you enter the temple itself.

There is a parallel floating walkway to the right, used while the main causeway was under repair. On the East side of the temple is a wide tree lined entrance which was added much later, and the stonework is crude. It is like the service entrance. The main ceremonial entrance is from the West.

The wide moat has stone retaining steps on either side to contain the soil. At points there are steps down to the water to access a boat. The upper three steps are sandstone and the lower three are laterite. The sheer amount of carved stone is staggering. But it is only the start.

Halfway over the bridge there are steps to the left and right down to the water and more Nagas and lions. Here you can also see the laterite layers underneath and the sandstone on top (as shown in Figure 2).

You cross the moat, the cosmic ocean from which the universe was born, and pass through one of five gates depending on your status. The large central gate was reserved for **Suryavarman II** alone. The gate to the right was for the Brahmin (priests) and on the left for senior court officials. The gates and the ends of the entrance to the left and right were for you and me, and wide enough for elephant to enter.

FIGURE 22: Boat landing stairs in Angkor moat

Go through the king's gate and next you walk on a raised stone walkway. You are at the earth level. At this stage you are still far from the actual temple and its mythical mountain. On either side are huge fields where crowds once gathered to see the king carried high on an elephant. The message is power and order. Think of a military parade ground or the long avenue in front of Versailles—wide, open, designed to humble the visitor. This is the first level.

Every now and then stairs lead down to the grassy fields, with more Nagas and lions. You pass by two small buildings—the "libraries" discussed earlier. Nearer the entrance to the main temple, you can walk down to two reflecting pools on either side. Take your iconic photo of Angkor from the wooden platform made for that purpose at the pool to the right.

You then take three sets of steps up to a wide raised platform known as the "Honour Terrace". You are at Level 2, in the realm of humans where stories of mankind and gods are intertwined. More Nagas and lions. To either side, the second outer wall wraps around the main temple and encloses a raised grass level. At either end of the temple, stairs lead up from the earth level. Continue and you reach your first shaded entrance with a little relief. This is still Level 2, the level of the carved friezes.

You enter a central junction with high ceilings. This is one of those major architectural focal points which is said to be "unfinished" because there are no decorations. Imagine it highly with various materials and decorated in gold and brilliant colours—a feast for the eyes.

In front of you are steps going to Level 3. It is not time to go there yet. It is time to see how human beings and gods interact. You will come back to this spot in about an hour after seeing the friezes.

To the left and right of this central junction are the corridors with the friezes. They form the next outer wall which wraps around the temple. Turn right and go through two vestibules necessary to support the structure above and then on to the first long corridor with a long frieze on the left. The ceiling is corbelled stone which once had a lower carved wooden ceiling. A section of the south corridor has been restored in this way. Later you will see from above that the roof above you looks like a snake wrapped around the temple.

This corridor which wraps around the whole temple is a sculpture gallery. These friezes were important to educate those who could not read the grand moral stories of their religion and their king's link to these. Think about the stained-glass windows in churches telling the stories of Jesus's life and Old Testament classics.

Walk all the way around this corridor and return to where you started. It is 804 metres long of which the friezes cover 520 metres. This is probably the biggest investment of time and brain power in your tour of Angkor, so don't rush. Take a snack bar or two and reward yourself at each corner! Once you have done your tour of the eight fascinating and hugely entertaining friezes, and two carved corner towers, you go up steps into Level 3.

This is the level of heavenly beings. Here you find a square with four sunken "pools" criss-crossed and surrounded by corridors with pillars and ceilings. And a large number of devatas standing guard.

Some speculate that these pools were for ritual cleaning for separate use by older and younger men, and older and younger women. This idea appears in older Hindu vastras (texts) on temple design, but no existing Hindu temple anywhere in the world has these. Some say they were for collecting rainwater which was then drained out of the temple. Some say the water collected was used to mix with other substances to wash statues according to Hindu customs.

The centre point of this level, a key focal point where a statue of **Vishnu** once stood, is also relatively bare of any decoration, at least in these times. Again, it is not necessarily unfinished, just undecorated. Surrounding this complex down at Level 2, is an inner grass courtyard and two more of these mysterious "libraries".

You then have a choice of three stairways up to Level 4. The central one is for the king, the one on the right for the priests, and on the left for senior court officials. These were the only people permitted to enter Level 4.

At Level 4 you reach another surrounding wall which is also a corridor. You can walk around and see the view outside from this level which is quite pleasant. You will pass by four large entrances on each of the four sides and glimpse a paved courtyard and the slopes of Mount Meru beyond.

These days there are statues of the historic Buddha at some points along this corridor—the focus of the simpler Theravada Buddhism—though originally there would have been stone, bronze (possibly silver or gold plated) statues of **Vishnu** himself or his most beloved avatars: **Krishna** and **Rama**. Incidentally, Vishnu adopts a new avatar each time the world falls into chaos and must be rebalanced between creation (**Brahma**) and destruction (**Shiva**).

In the middle of the paved courtyard, towering about the visitor is the main event: the summit of the holy mountain itself. The feeling all along is just like climbing a mountain: you think you're about to reach the top, only to find there is another stage to climb.

FIGURE 23: Angkor's central shrine, Level 5

Reaching Level 5 requires climbing incredibly steep stairs which are not for the faint-hearted. They are more like a rockface. The stairs for the king stick out further into the courtyard and are less steep. This is so that those carrying the king in his litter would not fall, and he with them!

You can't believe what is still to come as you climb up. Fortunately, there are new metal stairs with handrails built for today's visitors over the stone steps, but the climb up and down is still not for those who suffer from acrophobia. The reward is stupendous.

At Level 5, you are on the mountain top. You are in the home of the gods: the upper sanctuary. But like all mountain tops, you don't stand on a sharp point. You are on a large level which dips into four more squares of ponds, echoing that of Level 3. There is a rhythm of repetition, and you feel you have been here before.

FIGURE 24: (top) Gods on bridge to Angkor Thom

FIGURE 25: (bottom) Demons on bridge to Angkor Thom

In the middle is the central shrine to **Vishnu** approached from each direction of the compass. Far below this central sacred shrine is where the king's ashes were supposedly laid to rest. Today, there are statues of Buddha and a chance to light incense and make a small donation. A grill prevents people falling down into a pit (dug by French archaeologists looking for the funerary urn or any artifacts belonging to **Suryavarman II** as if he were a pharaoh: they found none). Walls were installed later so that from each direction of North, South, East and West you approached a statue of the Buddha.

Originally, a statue of **Vishnu** would have occupied the central position—either standing royally (my guess) or lying down in his pose giving rise to **Brahma** through his navel, who was in turn creating a new universe (not my guess since this is more about Brahma creating than Vishnu preserving).

The towers rise above the four corners of Level 5, with the fifth above the central shrine. They are the peaks of the perfect mountain (Mount Meru), the home of the gods and the centre of the Hindu universe. The feeling is like arriving in heaven after a long journey. The views from the surrounding corridor and corner vestibules outwards are spectacular, as they are from every part of Angkor, where you look outside to the jungle beyond.

Walk back through Angkor the way you came and take it all in again. On your way back to your *remorque* take some cold refreshment or a light meal at the tented restaurants on the right-hand side of the fields as you walk towards the entrance. The walk on that side is mostly shaded under large trees.

The breezy *remorque* ride to **Bayon** is through a leafy forest. Note the bridge railings over the moat as you enter Angkor Thom's walled city gates. As mentioned above, they have gods on the left and demons (Asuras) on the right all pulling the same snake, Vasuki, one way and then another. Also, you will see your first of the famous Bayon faces smiling at you over the entrance gate.

Bayon

You ride across the moat and through the gate tower towards the centre of Angkor Thom city, to the grand square dominated by the temple. You can walk up to Bayon from whatever cardinal direction you choose along on a short path. There are 20 staircases to the raised platform on which the whole temple rests. It is not like Angkor with its one central axis, one bridge over the moat from the West and one from the East.

Of the 20 staircases there is a bigger one in the centre of each of the four sides of the compass which takes you through the wall to the temple courtyard, but there is no sense of a differentiation by caste. Perhaps the other stairs were there for people to sit and chat and eat, watching others as they came and went.

The east entrance is slightly grander. You enter on an extended platform, originally covered near the entrance to the temple's inner courtyard. Nagas and lions are everywhere, though these lions are chunky and grinning, more Garfield than the slim lions at Angkor.

The ponds either side of the four main entrances represent the cosmic oceans. Once again, you are crossing from the earthly realm to the sacred realm; and they were handy for ritual washing and refreshment. You are on level one, in Buddhist terms, the world of humans.

Before walking through the wall to the inner courtyard, walk all the way around the temple on the

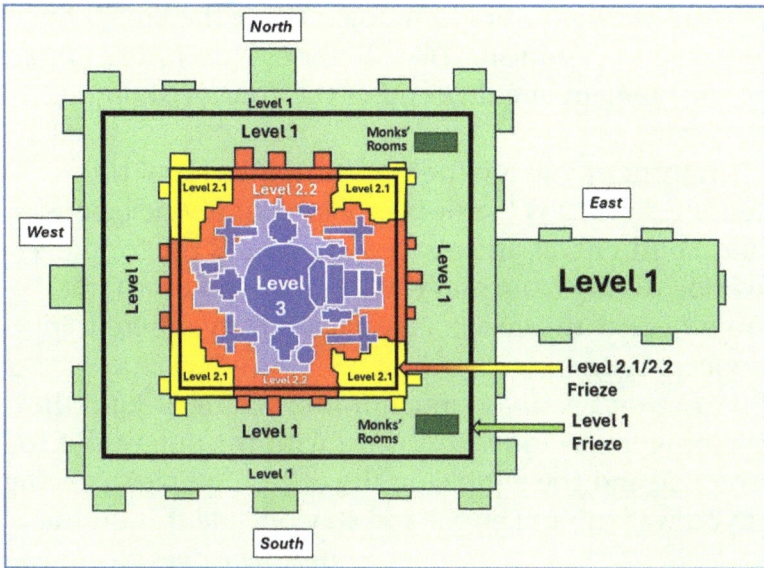

FIGURE 26: Plan view of Bayon Temple

outside to see the outer friezes. You will be watched by **Devatas**, some holding swords pointing down, meaning that they are okay with you entering. You will also be greeted by many **Apsaras** doing their "Bayon's Got Talent" audition mentioned before.

Originally you would have been in the shade as you walked around, though most of the roof has collapsed. Take your time to enjoy the friezes which are explained in the following section. They tell stories of recent battles and everyday life. They give Bayon the character of a city hall—the people's temple.

Arriving back at the east entrance after seeing the outer friezes, enter the courtyard through the outer wall at this level. As you step up, the courtyard level is below you on either side, and had many smaller buildings. A great many people were expected to be there at any one time visiting small shrines. The courtyard is wide and full of stones from past prayer buildings which were torn down when the kingdom reverted to Hinduism. Two "libraries" (multifunctional rooms) remain at either end of the courtyard on the east side.

In front of you are the two further levels of the temple. Level 2 is the heavenly land of divine beings and Bodhisattvas and above it, Level 3 is the formless world. Twenty staircases lead upwards on every side from Level 1 to Level 2. Once again, very different in concept to Angkor.

You won't gain too much from walking around the building in the inner courtyard with the outer walls to one side and the temple on the other. The view is better if you walk up to Level 2 and stay outside this on the narrow ledges around Level 2 and look down on the courtyard. There you can also enjoy the next set of friezes on the outside of the main building.

It is here that you start to understand the difference between Angkor and Bayon. Level 2 is in fact more than 20 different levels.

FIGURE 27: False door, Bayon Level 2.2

On the outside, a metre up here, three steps down, a step up, two steps down and so on. On the inside, 10 steps down there, 10 steps up again and multiple different levels.

Walking around the outside of the temple at this raised level is like hopping from rock to rock at the seaside. You can have fun trying to walk around—no need to go to the gym today. Having strong legs and not fearing heights helps. The friezes here are more of a religious nature, with a real mixing of Hindu and Buddhist images, defining Bayon's intent at fairness even in sacred matters.

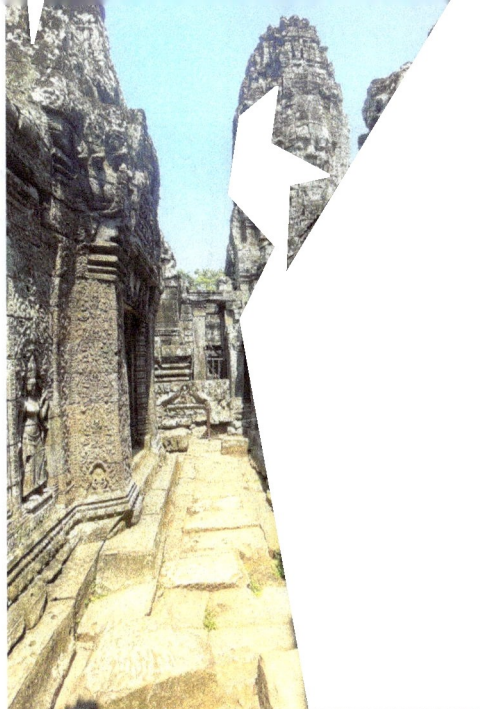

FIGURE 28: Bayon Passageway on Level 2.2 with view of faces

After seeing the friezes (explained in the next Chapter), you can enter the multi-level inside corridor at many different points. Inside, more passages veer off the main corridor at right angles with pillars on one side and walls on another. There are false doors in some parts carved in stone. You lose your sense of direction the moment you leave the main corridor and wander into the smaller inner passageways. This is not poor planning; it is design.

The easiest way not to get lost or go mad is to remember this: each corner of Level 2 is really the lowest part of Level 2—let's call it Level 2.1. From the big open courtyard on Level 1, there's just a short climb of stairs to get there. At Level 2.1, in each corner of

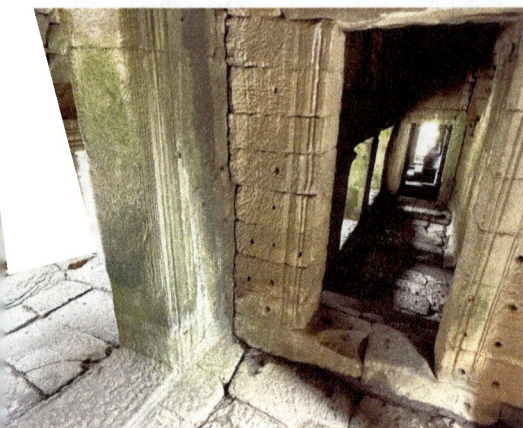

the building, you'll find a pleasant open courtyard and a small shrine for storing treasures or offering gifts and prayers. Look up, and you'll see the open sky—and maybe a few of those famous smiling faces watching you. Level 3 is still two floors higher, so don't start climbing yet.

As you walk inside along the main corridor going around the temple, towards the middle of each side of the temple, you go up another longer set of stairs—this is to Level 2.2. Now Level 3 is only one floor above your head.

FIGURE 29: Bayon stone maze at Level 2

FIGURE 30: Bayon Level 3: The Formless World

In this part of the building, space gets tight: small passages twist left and right like a stone maze, and you start to wonder if the builders were playing hide-and-seek. The space is taken up by big stone foundations supporting the terraces on Level 3, and the heads above. Some have false doors carved into them—they make it look like there are secret rooms hidden below the giant faces above. But don't be fooled. There's nothing behind them but solid laterite—just very clever stone pretending to be a door.

Bayon's many internal doorways, corridors, small courtyards, raised platforms and stairways say, "Welcome, from wherever you come. Have a seat, find some shade" Here, the temple feels like a market square or a parliament building, noisy with voices.

Five staircases, two on the East side and one on each of the others, then lead up to Level 3, the formless world. In the middle of Level 3 is an elaborate architectural crown, Level 4, with an extension to the east. The centre contained a statue of the Buddha. This statue was removed by later Hindu kings and buried but rediscovered and now is in a working outdoor temple nearby.

Surrounding the central crown, in a strangely asymmetric way, are those mysterious faces. This level has been closed to the public for several years for restoration but is open from 2026. I was fortunate to visit it a few times in 2019. It is richly carved in **Devatas** and **Apsaras**.

Walking around the faces is definitely an experience which strangely lifts your spirits. You cannot see who is around the corner so you are continually stepping aside or have others stepping aside for you, and everyone saying, "thank you", "sorry" and smiling politely.

When people smile at us, something is triggered in our brains which makes us smile back. At **Bayon**, the stones and the people are all smiling everywhere and you find yourself doing the same. Apparently smiling can trigger the release of serotonin, along with dopamine and endorphins, the brain's natural "feel-good" chemicals. Even a fake smile can send signals to your brain that lift mood slightly, reduce stress, and lower heart rate—which is why wandering among Bayon's endless serene faces might make you feel calmer and happier, even if you don't realise why. When you smile, you feel generous, even peaceful.

Angkor is a temple of religious teaching, heavenly beauty, order, overwhelming scale and restricted entrance. It is a religious journey to a mountain top.

Bayon is a complete contrast, a temple of welcoming inclusion, forcing contact between people whether you like it or not and a glimpse of peace and nirvana. It lifts you yet feels personal in scale totally unlike the cosmic scale of Angkor.

CHAPTER 8

THE FRIEZES: MOVIES IN STONE

The last part of this book is about the friezes—the stone stories that wrap around the temples. It's almost impossible to remember what they all mean before you go. This chapter is meant to be your friendly companion while you wander around the temples.

When you visit, one danger is that you might spend more time reading the tiny signboards than looking at the actual carvings. I've tried to make these stories more memorable, with a bit of wry humour to keep your eyes on the walls and your brain smiling.

Everyone looks at the friezes differently—some walk past quickly, some get lost for hours. Don't make the big mistake of rushing past the friezes—that's like going to a theatre and skipping the show! At least 30% of your visit to each temple should be spent walking slowly around the galleries at both temples.

To help you enjoy what you're looking at, I've kept things simple. First, I tell you the *big picture* of the frieze—what story it shows and what it means. Then I guide you from left to right, and sometimes top to bottom, so you don't get lost halfway through a battle between gods and demons. I point out the best "moments"—the real highlights. To help you find them, I've even counted the pillars opposite each moment, so you'll know exactly where to look.

My hope is that these pages help you pause a little longer, breathe in the carvers' skills and the beauty of their work, and see that these walls are not just old stone—they are stories carved for a king, but also for the people who lived, worked, and dreamed in his world. Every figure and every animal meant something to someone—from the gods and demons to the ruler on his elephant, the soldiers marching proudly and the farmer in his field. Eight hundred years later, their stories still speak, if we stop long enough to listen.

Stories which appear at both temples but in different ways

Four major Hindu stories appear at both temples— the **Churning of the Ocean of Milk** (twice at **Angkor**), the **Battle of the Gods and the Asuras (Demons)** and **Victory of Vishnu over the Demons** generally and **Victory of Krishna over Bana**.

Angkor tells these Hindu stories at a grand cosmic level. **Bayon** retells them through Buddhist compassion and realism. At Bayon, the line between good and bad is less clear—typical of **Jayavarman VII's** Buddhist view that all beings share both sides. Together, these temples argue in stone—one saying, "Respect the king", the other, "Look, this is life".

At **Angkor**, **Vishnu** and **Krishna** look like mighty warriors of the cosmos—stern, perfect, and ready for battle. At **Bayon**, you will see them with Buddhist symbols like the lotus, the dharma wheel, Buddhist hand gestures and serene faces, Bodhisattva-style crowns and jewellery. They've had spiritual training, sit a little quieter, smile a little softer, and seem ready to hand out life lessons instead of lightning bolts.

Angkor Friezes

The friezes at **Angkor** were once brightly painted and decorated, glowing in the tropical sun. Today almost all the colour has disappeared after nine centuries of sun and rain. In some way, we can appreciate them even more in the state their sculptors would have seen them before the painters moved in.

West Gallery, South Side—The Battle of Kurukshetra

You enter the temple from the Honour Platform and turn right. The first of the eight friezes is along this wall on your left. It is the **Battle of Kurukshetra**. The

FIGURE 31: Arjuna's soldiers with individual expressions march towards the battlefront

battle appears halfway through the massive Hindu epic *Mahabharata*. Imagine two families of cousins, the Pandavas and Kauravas, fighting a war to win control of the **Hastinapur** kingdom so big that even gods join in.

It's a story of duty before comfort because **Arjuna**, the great warrior of the **Pandava** family, *doesn't want to fight*. When he sees that many of his enemies are his own relatives and teachers, the **Kauravas**, including his beloved old mentor **Bhishma**, his heart breaks. He lowers his bow and says to Krishna, his charioteer, "How can I kill those I love?"

Krishna replies with calm wisdom and has a long discussion with Arjuna—this moment becomes the **Bhagavad Gita**, one of the most sacred texts in Hinduism. It is like a large "time out" in the middle of the battle as everyone else is frozen in action. He tells Arjuna that his duty (dharma) as a warrior is to *fight for justice*, not for pride or revenge. The soul, Krishna says, is eternal—it cannot be killed. Bhishma's body may fall, but his spirit continues. They talk about profound philosophical, ethical, and spiritual questions. Krishna offers guidance on how to live a righteous life and attain liberation. None of this is in the frieze; this is just for background.

In the battle, millions die, and the land is devastated. The battle is tragic and heroic and has meaning on many different levels. The carving at Angkor isn't just about battle—it's about the war inside every human heart: between what we want to do and what we must do.

I will present a little more detail for this first frieze because for me it is the best of the friezes in terms of overall artistic design. And the detailed design of the close entanglement of men, elephants, horses and chariots is incredible.

Look at either end of the frieze. There you can see the vertical legs of soldiers standing. Then further in from each side, they start to move towards the centre to the inevitable clash. Then they stand or kneel to throw spears. The middle half shows the clash between the two armies in a tangle of war animals, mounted soldiers and those on foot. There are similar layers above the eye-level layer which repeat the same action to show how wide the battlefront is.

There are **18 pillars** on your right. Opposite each pillar number you will see this:

Pillar 2: The is the Kauravas side of the frieze. The other end is the Pandavas. Arjuna's beloved mentor Bhishma lies on a bed of arrows deciding when to die (at the top of the frieze—away from the battlefield)

Pillar 3: The fighting starts. A Kauravas general on an elephant

Pillar 4: The Kauravas soldiers start running

Pillars 6–7: The first dead soldiers appear

Pillar 7: Someone looks like they have dropped their phone or keys and is frantically looking for them

Pillar 8: Someone is about to have their head chopped off

Pillar 9: Kauravas musicians keep the soldiers inspired or communicate commands using flutes and gongs

Pillars 9–10: Kauravas soldiers kneeling to throw spears

Pillars 10–11: Arjuna shooting an arrow and to the left of him the smaller figure of **Krishna** (who is really **Vishnu**). Presumably this is just before or just after the big time out for them to have their big ethical discussion (the **Bhagavad Gita**).

Pillars 13–14: Pandavas musicians with a gong to communicate commands

Pillar 14: Pandavas soldiers standing to throw spears. Pandavas general on a horse.

Pillar 16 and 17–18: Pandavas generals on horses.

Southwest Tower

The two western end corner towers of Angkor are like the temple's bonus chapters. Each tower has eight tucked-away large carved scenes above the windows. They feel almost like a director's cut for anyone who still has energy after the main movie. Most of the scenes are from the *Ramayana*, the famous epic love and rescue story which dominates culture in South and Southeast Asia.

As you enter start on the left and go around clockwise to see all eight scenes:

Scene 1: It all begins with a glittering distraction. **Rama** (the hero) sees a magical golden deer, really a demon in disguise, but he just wants to make **Sita** (his wife and heroine) happy. Off he runs into the forest, leaving her alone and setting off the world's most famous kidnapping by **Ravana**, the demon. Moral: never chase shiny things unless you're sure they're not cursed.

Scene 2: A sudden change of pace—no gods, no monsters, just royalty being royalty. Children wrestle, adults play chess, and courtiers gossip. It's the 12th-century version of "family time in the palace", proof that even royal households had noisy kids and unfinished chess games. And an outing on a boat.

Scene 3: This damaged panel still shows hints of palace life—a mix of dancers, musicians, and attendants. You can imagine laughter and rhythm once filling these walls.

Scene 4: In this panel, the calm trio of **Rama**, **Lakshmana** (his faithful brother), and **Hanuman** (their beloved monkey god supporter) anchor one corner while the chaos of the **Battle of Lanka** against the demon Ravana rages around them. The scene unfolds like a stone comic strip: monkey warriors hurl rocks and climb over elephants ridden by demons, Ravana's rakshasa army surges forward with clubs and spears, and Hanuman leads his troops with wild leaps and impossible strength. Above, Ravana, in his chariot with ten heads and twenty arms, fights furiously against Rama's divine arrows. In the end, the balance tips—the demons fall, the monkeys cheer, and the gods watch from the clouds as order and righteousness win the day.

Scene 5: **Shiva**, the great meditating god, shows what happens when you interrupt his peace. Along comes **Kama**, the god of love, armed with his flowery arrows, thinking he can make **Shiva** fall in love. Bad idea. One fiery glance later, Kama is turned to ashes—proof that even gods need quiet time and that romance can be hazardous near volcano-level temper.

Scene 6: The demon king **Ravana**, proud as ever, tries to lift the home of **Shiva** himself. The mountain quivers, gods panic, and probably wish they had insurance. **Shiva** stays still, then presses one toe to the ground—*slam!* Ravana is pinned like a fly under a sandal. Pride loses again, patience wins.

Scene 7: Opposite this drama stands **Parvati** (also called Uma), **Shiva**'s consort, clearly unimpressed. Hands on hips, she complains about **Ravana's** noise and arrogance—possibly also about her husband's endless calm. Every married couple will recognise the look.

Scene 8: To end, the great cosmic teamwork story: gods and demons tug a giant snake around a mountain to **churn the ocean of milk** and find the nectar of immortality. **Vishnu** manages the project, **Shiva** cleans up the poison, and everyone gets a good cosmic workout. It's the universe's first group project—and, miraculously, it worked. We will come to a whole frieze dedicated to this on the Southeast corridor.

The Southwest tower is a real mix of myths and stories. Maybe together they remind us that pride falls, patience wins, and even the gods have family problems and busy days.

South Gallery, West Side—The Procession of Suryavarman

Here you meet **Suryavarman II** face-to-face. But you don't just see a king—you travel back in time. This long, lively frieze is like a 12th-century newsreel, carved in stone. As you stand before it, you can almost step into the world that once filled the very fields you walked past on your way up to the Terrace of Honour. Eight hundred years ago, those open spaces outside the temple walls were alive with the same pageantry you see here.

From left to right there are two sections. Firstly, Suryavarman seated on a platform observing the procession below up to pillar 5. His concubines and chests with royal regalia are being carried to the platform. Next the procession takes up the whole height of the frieze until the end.

Later, in the middle of the frieze under the greatest number of umbrellas and being fanned, Suryavarman is riding an elephant. The procession includes 20 generals on elephants all evenly spaced like a good parade, and lieutenants on horseback as well as foot soldiers and courtiers. The weapons of war are scimitars and spears. Each regiment of soldiers has their own dress. It's easy to miss this detail.

You can almost hear the drums thumping, the pennants flapping, and the officials puffing in the heat, trying to look graceful while sweating through their linen. Everyone's focused, serious, and a little terrified—except Suryavarman, who looks like he's already planning his next temple. It's royal PR at its finest—a 12th-century power selfie. Every line and pose says: "I run the universe—and I do it with style".

FIGURE 32: A regiment of soldiers in Suryavarman II's parade in their individual battle dress and helmets

There are **38 pillars** on your right. Opposite each pillar number you will see this:

Pillars 1–2: The chief concubines being carried to the viewing platform

Pillars 3–4: The trunks under umbrellas aren't picnic baskets—they're the royal "suitcases of the sacred", containing items like betel boxes and royal clothing and crown jewels, possibly Suryavarman's armour to change into for the parade. A betel box was the medieval Cambodian handbag of hospitality—part breath freshener, part energy boost, part fashion statement. Everyone from kings to grandmothers carried one, and after a few chews, everyone smiled with bright red teeth.

Pillar 4: The famous portrait of **Suryavarman II** seated on the viewing platform to watch the parade. You will notice that all gods wear the same crown as his—that's how you can identify them later when they are all mixed up fighting the demons.

Pillars 5–6: Descending from the viewing platform to the parade field

Pillars 20–21: **Suryavarman II** in the parade with the most parasols and fans and just after him, the standard bearing **Vishnu and Garuda**

Pillars 27–28: The sacred flame that signified the king's right to rule

After this frieze there is a gate entrance from the fields of Level 1 running through the corridor and out the other side which divide the corridors on every side into two.

South Gallery, East Side—Heaven and Hells

Here the stone carvers clearly had fun—and maybe a touch of mischief. This is the heaven and hell of Hindu belief.

At the top sits **Yama**, the god of justice, calmly riding his bull and keeping score. Around him, the lucky souls float upward to heaven—fine clothes, smiles, good posture. Below them, things get … hotter. The sinners tumble into pits, get chewed by monsters, are boiled for their bad behaviour or have spikes driven into them as their bodies are stretched by heavy weights. It's the ancient world's version of a warning poster: be good, or prepare to be barbecued.

FIGURE 33: People pushed through the gate of hell towards punishment

The detail is amazing—heaven looks palatial, peaceful and graceful. Hell looks like a very bad day at work. Together they remind us that Suryavarman's perfect order extended beyond this life too: paradise for the obedient, punishment for the reckless.

The concept of hell in Hinduism is different to that of Christianity—it is not forever, thank goodness. When a person dies, Yama looks at their life record— like a divine customs officer. If you've been kind and honest, your soul goes to one of the many heavens. If you've been cruel, greedy, or lazy, you spend some time in Naraka, where the punishment fits the crime—liars might have their tongues pulled, thieves might walk on hot coals, and the proud might fall headfirst into mud.

But here's the key: once your soul has learned its lesson, you're reborn. There's no eternal damnation— just spiritual correction, like cosmic detention class.

In short, Hindu hell isn't forever—it's more like a temporary afterlife boot camp run by Yama, the strict but fair headmaster of karma.

Initially the frieze has three levels—the obviously good at the top, those seeking to purify themselves in the middle by consulting and bringing offerings to priests and priestesses and below them, people doing cruel things to other human beings, like leading groups of what seems like slaves with hooks in their noses. The frieze is then dramatically altered at the gates of hell, the turning point.

After that, there are only two levels separated by a thin decorative band of eagles and lions. At the top is heaven which looks like a series of hotel rooms with happy guests and quality curtains. Hell is below where what takes place makes Hieronymus Bosch's famous paintings look like a picnic in the park.

There are **26 pillars** on your right. Opposite each pillar number you will see this:

Pillars 2–3: People seem to be consulting priests and priestesses and offering gifts, trying to live good lives to make it to heaven

Pillars 6–7: **Yama** on his bull giving judgement

Pillars 8–9: The gates of hell with people being pushed down and the fire of hell

Pillar 19: Man being boiled in a pot

Pillars 19–20: Spiky trees to torture people and then burn them

Pillars 25–26: Someone having their eyeball poked out with a long stick

Pillar 26 to the end: Some bad folk being stretched out with weights either vertically or over a pole, and then spikes being hammered into their bodies

The Southeast tower has no decoration, but the views are great, and it connects with the staircase up from the East side of Angkor for common people. Just after this if you look out the first window and to your right you can see the unfinished Devata and window frame mentioned earlier.

East Gallery, South Side—The Churning of the Ocean of Milk (A Cosmic Smoothie Machine)

This wall tells one of the greatest stories ever imagined—the **Churning of the Ocean of Milk**, known in Sanskrit as *Samudra Manthana*. Here, 88 gods pull backwards and forwards on one end of the giant snake **Vasuki** and 92 demons on the other. They use it as a rope. The poor snake is wrapped around **Mount Mandara**, which spins in the middle of the cosmic ocean as they pull back and forth like a giant eggbeater. At the centre of it all, **Vishnu** is the project manager, keeping the snake from slipping off the mountain. He has turned round to face you, as if posing for a photograph. Beneath it all, Vishnu appears again—this time as a **turtle**, calmly holding the mountain on his shell so it doesn't sink.

As the churning begins, the cosmic milk which is the universe before creation, starts to bubble and foam, and all kinds of treasures rise to the surface—jewels, Apsaras (see **Figure 7**), **amrita** (the nectar of immortality) and even poison, which **Vishnu** coolly swallows. The gods tricked the demons and made sure they got first share of the amrita and the demons had to wait at the end of the line.

So, what does it mean?

You can't reach immortality or enlightenment without stirring the depths—good and evil, pleasure and pain, working together to bring truth to the surface. It's a story about effort, teamwork, and a touch of divine trickery—a cosmic smoothie made by two sides who can't stand each other yet needed each other to reach immortality.

There are three levels—the creatures of the ocean at the bottom, the gods and demons in the middle and at the top, flocks of apsaras being released into the cosmos.

There are **19** pillars on your right. Opposite each pillar number you will see this:

- **Pillars 2:** A well-known demon Tatukan and the head of the snake **Vasuki**
- **Pillars 4–5**: Another well-known demon Tusakan
- **Pillar 9:** The main event where **Vishnu** is supervising the churning operation in the middle of it all

- **Pillars 13–14:** A "good" demon on the side of the gods— like a politician who changed parties
- **Pillars 15–16:** The god **Brahma**, creator of the universe
- **Pillars 18:** The god **Hanuman**—the monkey god famed for his loyalty, courage and strength and hero of the *Ramayana*.

Then the corridor is intersected by the vestibules carrying the structure of the entrances from the East. The middle for the king and either side for priests and court officials or aristocrats. Look for the wooden lintel above the entrance after the main king's entrance. Think of the wooden decoration which would have greeted you here.

At either end of this East side of the temple, where the towers are, there are entrances for the common people. There are several vestibules to carry the weight of the structures above these entrances.

East Gallery, North Side—Vishnu's Victory Over the Asuras

This frieze was begun and finished around 1564, 400 years after those we have just seen. Here, you can see **Vishnu's** great victory over the Asuras—the demons who never quite learned when to give up. Vishnu rides his flying bird, **Garuda**, like a superhero on a jetpack, leading his army of gods into battle. Below him, the Asuras charge forward, all teeth, muscles, and bad manners. The gods look calm and organised—the Asuras look like they forgot the battle plan.

Arrows fly, spears clash, and in the middle Vishnu keeps his cool, aiming perfectly while the world goes wild around him. You can almost hear him saying, "Honestly, how many times do I have to save the universe?"

It's a scene of cosmic order beating chaos—a bit like a tidy teacher winning against a noisy classroom. And carved with such precision that even the chaos looks beautifully planned.

What does it all mean?

Vishnu's role in Hindu belief is to protect the universe whenever evil grows too strong. The demons, the Asuras, stand for greed, pride, and confusion. The gods, or Devas, stand for truth, duty, and balance. Every time the balance tips too far, Vishnu steps in—sometimes as himself, sometimes as one of his avatars like Rama or Krishna—to set things right.

This battle isn't just about who wins; *it's about the constant need to restore balance in the world and in ourselves.*

Here is something else interesting. There are 20 pillars on your right. Why not 19 like the previous gallery with the Churning of the Ocean of Milk? Why was it a bit longer?

If you think the optical tricks of the Parthenon in Athens are impressive, the Khmer builders were playing the same genius game. Because Cambodia sits just north of the equator, the sunlight falls mostly from right to left during the day looking from the West. This made the right-hand side look brighter—and therefore a little bigger.

So, what did the Khmer architects do? They added one extra pillar on the left to balance the illusion. A perfect solution: part geometry, part psychology, part genius.

They didn't need to do this on the north and south sides, and the east side—well, that wasn't the star of the show anyway. It simply followed the west façade's clever lead.

The carving on this gallery and the one following were completed in 1564, during the decline of the

Khmer Empire. This was about 400 years after the previous carvings were completed. The effect is not as three-dimensional, and the design is less complex. Although they are still impressive, they are not in the same class artistically and technically as those we have already seen.

Between **pillars 6–7** is a beautifully decorated horse. And between **pillars 10–11** you can see the hero **Vishnu** on **Garuda**.

The Northeast tower is a mirror of the Southeast tower and has no decoration and is the vestibule at the top of the steps from grass level.

North Gallery, East Side—Krishna's Victory Over the Asura Bana (Banasura)

This frieze was also begun and completed around 1564. Here, the beloved hero Krishna (an avatar or earthly form of **Vishnu** visiting earth in human form) takes centre stage in his battle with **Banasura**, a demon king who made the mistake of having too many arms and too much confidence. It is more personal and focused than the grander scenes of Vishnu fighting the demons.

Here, Krishna rides proudly on his mighty bird Garuda, eight arms flying like windmill blades—every hand holding a weapon and every strike perfectly aimed. Below, Banasura's army charges in confusion, a sea of flailing limbs and panic. It's hard to tell where one demon ends and the next begins—like a badly organised football team.

In the next scene, Krishna has already won *but still shows mercy*. The defeated Banasura kneels, while a group of powerful gods including **Shiva** and **Brahma** (**Vishnu-level** gods) politely recommend that Krishna not kill him. A good reason is that *Banasura is devoted to Shiva*! Krishna, ever the gentleman, agrees not to smite a fellow god's devotee—and shows a god knows both power, compromise and restraint. Krishna fights not just to win, but to teach us all about humility and mercy.

It's a comic-book moment in stone: hero, villain, victory, forgiveness—all carved with the drama of an epic film, yet quiet enough that you can almost hear Krishna saying, "Okay … enough already".

The whole scene progresses from left to right with many appearances of Krishna and Garuda in action. At the end Banasura appears followed by the group of gods mentioned above deliberating whether he should be killed or not.

There are **26 pillars** on your right. Opposite each pillar number you will see this:

Pillars 2–3: Krishna with Garuda

Pillar 4: Garuda having a moment of his own protecting Krishna from the fire with his wings of metal

Pillar 4–5: A demon riding a rhino. Why a rhino? Because it symbolises brute power and stubbornness. Some have called this demon **Mahishasura**, but it is not him—he belongs to a different story. This demon has similar features, but it was a case of **Khmer** artists borrowing ideas from other Hindu myths for their design. At this stage, the **Khmer Empire** was predominantly the simpler Theravada Buddhism with only pockets of Hindu traditions.

Pillars 9–10: This is Krishna, but unlike we have seen him before. Now he has multiple heads. These changes were common at that time where the strict representation of each god varied. They call it syncretic—when two religions meet, can't decide who's right, and end up sharing temples, festivals, and the same confused worshippers—a kind of divine "fusion cuisine".

What could change from stricter earlier forms: the number of heads, the hairstyle, the type of headdress or crown, the necklaces, clothing, especially the number of arms and what was in each hand and being seated or standing.

Pillars 12–13: Gods in a heavenly boat riding in the cosmic ocean, helping Krishna—like his heavenly navy

Pillars 15–16: Krishna and Garuda again

Pillar 18: Krishna and Garuda again

Pillars 20–21: Krishna and Garuda again

Pillars 22–23: Banasura (also called Vana) with his 22 arms

Pillars 24–end: Krishna and Garuda again and **Shiva**, and his sons **Ganesha** (the Elephant) and **Iskandar** (or Murugan, Kartikeya) and **Parashurama** with his axe. He is the 6th avatar of **Vishnu** who received his axe from Shiva after saying sorry for cutting off one of Ganesha's tusks. Then there is **Brahma** with the long beard. They are all giving Krishna advice. The Apsaras below them indicate that this discussion is happening in the realm of the gods.

You pass through the vestibules linked to the entrance from the North.

North Gallery, West Side—Gods versus Asuras

In this next frieze **Vishnu** isn't alone. It's the whole heavenly team—all the gods joining forces against the demons. It's like the mythological version of the Avengers. Everyone has a weapon, everyone's shouting, and nobody quite remembers who started the fight. It shows the eternal struggle between light and darkness, chaos and order—a theme found across Hindu stories.

Here, twenty-one gods charge into battle, led again by the ever-cool **Vishnu**, riding his Garuda like a one-man air force. Around him the gods keep their lines neat and their faces calm, while the **Asuras**, all fangs and fury, look like they missed the rehearsal.

Weapons fly, bodies twist, and the stone almost seems to shake with noise—yet **Vishnu** remains unruffled, perfectly balanced while chaos breaks loose below. It's a battle of good manners versus bad temper, and once again the calm side wins.

The overall design of the frieze is the gods starting in the East and the demons starting in the West and the clash happening all along. The demons are mostly riding Nagas.

There are **38 pillars** on your right. Opposite each pillar number you will see this:

Pillars 11–12: Meet **Kubera** the god of money riding on **Yaksha**

Pillar 15: **Shiva**'s son **Iskandar** (the god of war) on his peacock mount. Unusually he has multiple heads.

Pillar 18: The god **Indra** on his famous elephant **Airavata**, shown here with four tusks

Pillar 21: **Banasura** on a five headed Naga

Pillars 22–23: **Vishnu** on Garuda

Pillars 29–30: **Iskandar** again on his peacock

Pillars 29–30: **Varuna**, the sea god, riding a makara (like a scary duckbill platypus)

Pillars 31–32: The moon god **Chandra**

Pillars 36–37: A lion fighting a tiger.

The northwest tower and the West gallery following is pure drama in stone—once again, the *Ramayana.*

Vishnu is the director. In the tower is the trailer. In the gallery that follows is they key action scene in the drama.

In the tower, starting on the left and going clockwise:

Scene 1: Enter **Vishnu**, the cosmic protector, soaring through the heavens on his mighty bird Garuda. Garuda looks half eagle, half superhero, carrying his master as if late for a divine meeting. It's a grand entry—feathers flying, demons scattering.

Scene 2: This is no ordinary sports day—it's an archery contest for the hand of a princess. The challenge: string the huge divine bow that no mortal can lift and shoot an arrow through a ring. Many princes try and fail, but **Rama**, **Vishnu**'s human avatar, strings it effortlessly. The bow even snaps—a romantic mic drop.

Scene 3: **Vishnu** sits high in the Himalayas, eyes closed in calm meditation. The world below buzzes, but he stays still—until word comes that **Indra** needs a son-in-law for his daughter **Sita**. **Vishnu** smiles—time to take human form as **Rama** and make some divine romance happen.

Scene 4: Now the mood changes. Enter **Ravana**, the ten-headed demon king, surrounded by his advisors. They're not planning a surprise party—they're scheming to steal Rama's sacred bow and arrow. Every good story needs a villain, and Ravana clearly loves his job.

Scene 5: Here we see **Hanuman**, the monkey general, loyal, brave, and bursting with energy. He and his troops crowd around Rama in the royal palace, ready for orders. You can almost hear the chatter—tails twitching, plans flying. It's the divine army's team meeting before the great rescue mission.

Scene 6: This is one of the most emotional scenes. After being rescued from Ravana, Sita must prove her purity (that she has not been violated by Ravana) by stepping into the fire. Flames rise—but instead of burning, they bless her. The fire god himself (**Agni**) declares her spotless. Rama's face shows relief—and perhaps a note to self: trust your wife next time.

Scene 7: The gods gather as the story comes full circle. **Indra**, **Rama**, **and Sita** discuss their divine union above—while below, the chaos unfolds as *Ravana kidnaps Sita*. It's love, loss, and heavenly paperwork all carved into stone.

Scene 8: Finally, a calm ending. **Vishnu** reclines on the great serpent **Ananta** (or Shesha), floating on the cosmic ocean. From his navel rises a lotus flower, and on that lotus sits **Brahma**, ready to create the universe. It's the Hindu circle of life: from rest comes creation—proof that even the gods need a nap before big projects.

This tower may be small, but it's packed with love, loyalty, jealousy, and forgiveness—proof that long before movies and novels, the best drama was already being written in sandstone.

West Gallery, North Side—The Battle of Lanka

Here the same characters from the northwest tower appear in full blockbuster level with the Battle of Lanka—the main action scene from the *Ramayana*, where Rama (another avatar of **Vishnu**) takes on the demon king **Ravana** to rescue his wife, **Sita**. It's the highlight of the movie before everything is wrapped up at the end.

The overall design from left to right is preparation for the battle, then the chaos of the battle and then the doom of Ravana just before he thinks he can escape.

The scene is a wild storm of energy—monkeys leap, demons roar, and arrows fill the sky. Rama's army, led by the heroic Hanuman, charges across the wall like an army of acrobats, tails flying and muscles carved in perfect mid-jump. Ravana, the ten-headed villain, sits proudly in his chariot, waving his many weapons at once—a clear case of *too many heads, not enough sense*.

Everywhere you look, the stone is alive: bridges made of monkey bodies, war elephants in panic, and soldiers tumbling in artistic defeat. Rama, cool and focused, draws his divine bow—one arrow, one purpose—while Hanuman watches adoringly.

It's the ancient world's action movie, a tale of love, loyalty, and friendship—and proof that even in the 12th century, good storytelling and good carving never go out of style.

There are 20 pillars on your right. Opposite each pillar number you will see this:

- Pillars 8–9: In the middle of the battle, Rama rides on Hanuman's shoulders while Lakshmana fights beside him. When a noble demon named Vibhishana, Ravana's brother, joins Rama's side, Rama tells his army, "Don't kill the demons who are only obeying orders". Even in war, he shows mercy—fighting evil leaders, not the ordinary soldiers.
- Pillar 10: Throughout this frieze you have two separate moments captured together—a bit like "how it started" and "how it ended". You see a

monkey attacking the animal pulling the chariot and then he attacks the person riding in the chariot.

- **Pillars 10–11: Vali,** one of the most powerful fighters in the world kills a demon commander and a lion as well
- **Pillars 12–13:** Ravana, the demon king
- **Pillars 14–15: Nikumbha,** one of Ravana's generals, rides a buffalo but is taken down in one blow by Hanuman.

Bayon Friezes

Bayon has friezes on the four sides of Level 1 and the same on Level 2.

Spend more time on the Level 1 friezes. They are more complete and easier to view. These friezes show battles, more battles, markets, and monkeys stealing lunch.

The second level walls are different. They are religious, showing gods, Buddhas, and peace at last.

The Bayon friezes are a lot shorter than those at Angkor and involve less grand storytelling. The reason may be architectural since the temple is smaller in design and the corridors at Level 1 are interrupted by elaborate entrances. At Level 2, it is even more problematic since the many staircases break up the friezes into small sections.

There is something in every metre of these friezes to reward you with life, laughter, and history. It isn't just an art display—it's a Cambodian movie, complete with comedy, patriotism, compassion and action sequences. That said, there's a clear difference in quality between these carvings and the ones at Angkor. They appear to be made in less time, with less depth and the illusion of being three-dimensional.

The **Apsaras** are a real delight. They're on pillars everywhere, each one or pair or trio striking a different pose, and worth admiring for their balance alone.
At the main entrances, you may also notice a few **Devatas**—calm, watchful guardians making sure you behave yourself.

The Bayon friezes are not described here in the same detail as those of Angkor. Some parts are very rough or worn—perhaps because they've been far more exposed to wind and rain than those at Angkor. Many are faint, or partly missing, and in some cases the gods have been deliberately defaced by later followers of other faiths. Rather than guessing at every uncertain scene and giving multiple possibilities, I have given only a broad outline of their subjects—this is not Angkor's clear storytelling in stone, but you can still enjoy the fragments and imagine your own version of the story as you walk along the walls.

Level One

East Gallery—The March Begins (Another Bayeux Tapestry, Khmer Style)

The story starts with a **Khmer** army on the move, marching proudly across the wall as if late for a parade. There are elephants, horsemen, drummers, and wagons full of supplies—even a few Chinese soldiers and mounted officers helping out, their chignon hairstyles neatly carved. The rhythm of the parade feels musical; you can almost hear the rhythmic clatter of hooves and the occasional elephant sneeze.

On the next wall, the soldiers give way to village life. You'll see **Khmer** wooden houses on stilts, merchants at work, and yes—Chinese traders again, maybe selling silk or tea. It's a rare, lively glimpse of what daily life looked like 800 years ago—business, gossip, and business deals.

South Gallery—Boats, Battles, and a Busy Market

Now things heat up—literally and historically. The southern gallery bursts into life with a naval battle on the Tonle Sap Lake. You can spot **Khmer** boats colliding with **Cham** ships, spears flying, warriors shouting, and one poor soldier about to fall overboard. Beneath the battle, a market scene unfolds, where vendors weigh fish and bargain for fruit—possibly wondering if the noise above means higher seafood prices.

Past the doorway, the story continues with fishermen casting nets, a proud Chinese junk sailing by, and even a cockfight below—early Cambodian entertainment! Then, you'll see palace scenes with princesses and servants chatting, wrestlers locked in combat, and even a wild boar fight for good measure. After that comes another battle, the **Cham** storming ashore while **Khmer** warriors protect themselves with shields made of coiled rope—the ancient version of bubble wrap. The Khmer win, of course, and the next scene shows the king's victory feast, complete with musicians, dancers, and everyone pretending the war was easy.

At the far west of this gallery, the army marches again—**Khmer** and **Cham** together, with elephants, catapults, and a giant crossbow that looks like something a genius teenager might have built.

West Gallery—Unfinished Business and Wild Ideas

Here the carving gets patchy—some sections unfinished, others half-polished, as if the artists ran out of time or got called to dinner. You'll see soldiers marching through a forest, then **Khmer** arguing and

FIGURE 34: People kneading and turning out bread

fighting among themselves—proof that politics has always been messy.

North Gallery—Entertainment and Aftermath

The north side begins with a wonderful scene of royal entertainment—acrobats, jugglers, and athletes showing off their tricks while musicians play nearby. This reminds me of the wonderful **Phare Circus** which you can see nightly in **Siem Reap**. Behind them, you'll see processions of animals and holy men meditating in the forest, which feels like Cambodia's first outdoor festival.

Then the story shifts—more battles between the **Khmer** and **Cham**, warriors in tight ranks clashing across the stone. In one section, the Khmer are fleeing, clearly not their best day at work, while the Chams advance with determination. But don't worry—they'll win on the next wall!

Finally, in the northeast corner, another **Khmer** army marches again, steady and proud, and in the eastern gallery, a last grand land battle unfolds: elephants on both sides charging like thunder. The Khmer have the upper hand, and the story ends—as all royal carvings should—with their victory carved forever in stone.

Bayon Level Two

As noted above, climbing up to the second level of Bayon feels less like visiting a temple and more like joining an adventure sport. The outer walkways turn and drop without warning—a rock rabbit's dream, a mountain goat's gym, and a tourist's test of balance. But if you're brave (and reasonably flexible), this level rewards you with some of the most beautiful and mysterious Hindu scenes in the Angkor area. Unlike the big outer galleries, these are smaller, more personal friezes—moments of myth rather than massive parades.

There is less attempt to show real depth or perspective. The artist is thinking more like a designer than a painter. It's similar to how, in modern art, painters began to move away from showing the world realistically and instead focused on patterns, shapes, and rhythm—as if the picture were meant to decorate rather than describe.

The second level of Bayon is not about size or spectacle—it's about sacred storytelling on a human scale. The carvings show Hindu gods and heroes amid Buddhist symbols, sometimes clear, sometimes mysterious, but always alive with energy. Unlike the noisy outer friezes below, these are quieter conversations between gods, kings, and fate.

You may find yourself the only person having a look at these friezes since most people go straight into the building.

Begin in the middle of the east side. The first thing you notice is how uneven the wall surface is—as if the sculptors worked fast or never came back to polish.

The carvings here are small narrative panels rather than one long parade. Many scholars think they were added later under **Jayavarman VIII**, who tried to restore Hinduism after **Jayavarman VII**'s Buddhist reign.

South Gallery—Shiva on a Lotus and the Gods at Work

Moving along the south side (mind your step—it dips and rises like a stony rollercoaster), you'll find a calmer, more elegant scene: **Shiva** seated peacefully on a lotus flower. Around him, Apsaras flutter like carved butterflies, and nearby are images of **Vishnu** and **Brahma**, completing the sacred Trimurti, the three great gods of Hinduism.

FIGURE 35: Patient receiving hospital care

The mood here is quiet, meditative—as if the temple wanted to take a deep breath after all the fighting and politics below. The carvings are more delicate, the gods looking serene and slightly amused, perhaps watching climbers below trying to keep their balance on the uneven walkway.

West Gallery—The Churning of the Ocean of Milk

As you turn the corner, the carvings become clearer. This section holds that most famous story in Hindu myth—**The Churning of the Ocean of Milk.**

It's smaller and shallower than the grand version at Angkor, but the scene is unmistakable: gods and demons pulling the serpent **Vasuki** in a cosmic tug-of-war, with **Vishnu** steadying the mountain on his turtle avatar below.

The detail is sketchy now—the serpent's coils barely visible—but the rhythm of movement remains. You can almost feel the pull, the teamwork, the chaos. It's a scene about cooperation between enemies—a fitting theme for a temple that mixes Hindu and Buddhist ideas so freely.

Further along, another set of figures shows craftsmen at work, perhaps building a temple. It's one of the few times the builders themselves appear in stone, a quiet tribute to the hands that carved all of this.

North Gallery—The Heroes of the Mahabharata

Now heading back toward the east, the carvings fade even more, as if retreating into shadow. Yet this side holds the echoes of another great epic—scenes from the *Mahabharata*, the story of family war and moral duty.

You can just make out lines of warriors, bows drawn, and a few elephants mid-charge. In one section, a wise old figure reclines on a bed—perhaps **Bhishma**, the dying general whose lessons outlived him. The carving is faint but knowing what it once showed helps the imagination fill the gaps.

East Gallery—The North Side

You are back on the side you started. A little way along you find the story of "The Leper King". The first scene shows a king fighting a giant serpent with his bare hands—impressive, but risky. The next panel shows the king's hands being examined by worried attendants and women, perhaps looking for poison wounds. Finally, the poor man lies in bed, clearly unwell, wrapped in royal blankets but looking less than royal. According to the legend, the serpent's venom gave him leprosy, and his sad fate earned him the title "The Leper King".

Some scholars say it could also show a goddess freed from a mountain, or maybe **Cham** invaders destroying idols—nobody's quite sure. Either way, it's a fascinating mix of faith, illness, and mystery carved into stone. The message seems to be that even kings should think twice before wrestling snakes.

CHAPTER 9

TOURING TIPS

How to See Without Sighing

After all the stories of kings, gods, and carvings, here's the real question: how do you tour Angkor and Bayon without getting bored or too tired? A few tricks can make the difference between "not another temple" and "that was amazing".

1. **Save your strength.** Many visitors charge into Angkor Wat at sunrise like it's a race—and by mid-morning they look ready to lie down at the hotel swimming pool. You don't need to be one of them, squinting into the bright sun at sunrise and nursing a headache before breakfast.

   Take it easy: enjoy your breakfast and coffee first and start around 8 a.m. If you plan well, you can explore Angkor until about 10:30, stop for a snack and a cold drink, and still have plenty of energy left for Bayon. That's the perfect time of day—when the crowds are smaller, and those giant stone faces seem to smile just for you.

2. **Rest like a king.** In the old days, kings had shaded pavilions and servants with fans. You don't—but there is plenty of shade inside the temples. In between the two temples, buy a cold coconut.

3. **Grab a Meal between Angkor and Bayon.** These are outdoor, with one or two airconditioned restaurants dotted around the archaeological sites. I have always had delicious meal at any of them. If you walk down the right-hand side towards the entrance at Angkor, you will be under the shade of giant trees.

4. **Compare as you go.** At each carving or tower, ask yourself: "Is this Angkor energy or Bayon energy?" Is it formal, grand, and polished? That's Angkor. Is it lively, a bit confusing, and human? That's Bayon. This game keeps your eyes sharp and your brain awake.

5. **Keep your humour.** Remember: this was once theatre as much as temple. Angkor was the king's stage set, Bayon the people's stage. Walk with that in mind, and even when you are hot and sweaty, you will feel the story pulling you along.

Final Thought

At the start of this book, I wrote: "These two temples are like two sides of the same human heart. Angkor shows the side that respects reverence, ambition, and stability. Bayon shows the side that loves life, fairness, and compassion. Both are part of who we are."

Maybe that's the real message carved in the stone—that life, like the temples, stands strongest when stability and compassion hold hands.

As you leave the jungle and head for that cool hotel pool, perhaps the secret is not about choosing one side, but learning to see beauty and value in both.

A Short (and Sometimes Chaotic) History of Mainland Southeast Asia, 0–1250 CE

Long before tourists arrived with cameras and guidebooks, mainland Southeast Asia was already alive with activity. Kingdoms rose, traded, prayed, and, quite often, fought. The region was a busy crossroads of ideas and ambition—a meeting place of great rivers, powerful kings, and very different cultures trying to live side by side.

Around 0 CE, Indian traders and monks began sailing to the coasts of what we now call **Cambodia**, **Vietnam**, and **Thailand**. They did not come as conquerors but as teachers and merchants. From India came Hindu gods, Buddhist monks, new scripts and languages, and, perhaps most influential of all, the belief that a king could also be divine. Local rulers liked this idea—it gave their crowns a heavenly sparkle.

By about 500 CE, the **Khmer** people were farming the fertile plains around the great **Tonle Sap Lake**. Their early kingdoms—**Funan** and later **Chenla**—grew in power and sophistication. By 800 CE, a king named **Jayavarman II** united them and founded **Angkor**, the future heart of the **Khmer Empire**. The Khmer became the master builders of Southeast Asia. Their kings measured greatness not by years ruled, but by the size of their temples. If satellites had existed, Angkor would have been visible from space—a statement of faith, power, and perhaps healthy royal ego.

To the East, along the coast of central **Vietnam**, lived the **Cham**, a seafaring people of Indian influence who worshipped **Shiva** and built graceful red-brick temples at **My Son** (near modern day **Da Nang**). They were traders, sailors, and occasionally pirates, ruling the seas and controlling coastal trade between India, China, and the Khmer. They admired beauty but also enjoyed raiding—especially Khmer cities. For centuries, the Khmer and the Cham behaved like strong neighbours separated by too little distance and too much pride. Sometimes they exchanged goods and sometimes arrows.

Their rivalry lasted almost 600 years. The most dramatic moment came in 1177, when **Cham** war canoes sailed up the **Mekong River** to the **Tonle Sap Lake**, stormed **Angkor**, and looted the capital. The **Khmer** world was stunned. Then came their answer—**Jayavarman VII**, a Buddhist king and a man of action. He rebuilt Angkor as Angkor Thom and crowned it with the **Bayon** temple, whose smiling stone faces seemed to forgive but not forget. The **Cham** were defeated so completely that later visits were likely for trade or coconuts rather than conquest.

Meanwhile, new people were arriving from the north—the **Tai**, ancestors of today's **Thai** and **Lao**. Originating in the hills of southern **China**, they drifted southward, building small kingdoms in the river valleys of what is now northern **Thailand** and **Laos**. At first, they paid tribute to the mighty **Khmer**, learning their architecture, religion, and art. But, like good students, they soon became competitors. By 1250 CE, the Thai kingdom of **Sukhothai** was rising, and the Khmer were discovering how it felt to have lively neighbours on all sides.

To the far north, **China** watched with both interest and caution. The great dynasties preferred trading silk and collecting tribute to sending armies through steamy jungles. Between China and the Khmer stood Dai Viet, the state of northern Vietnam—smart, disciplined, and ambitious. It had inherited Chinese-style government but kept its Southeast Asian independence. The Dai Viet often fought the Cham, sometimes allied with the Khmer, and occasionally annoyed both—showing that politics was already Southeast Asia's favourite sport.

By 1250 CE, the map looked something like this:

- The Khmer Empire remained vast but weary from its own greatness.

- The Cham were still proud but fading from the stage.

- The Thai were young, confident, and about to make history of their own.

- The Dai Viet held firm in the north, and the Chinese and Indians kept sending ideas instead of soldiers.

It was a region alive with competition, belief, and brilliance—a place where kingdoms rose from rice fields and ideas travelled faster than armies.

A Short (and Sometimes Still Chaotic) History of Mainland Southeast Asia, 1250–2025 CE

By 1250 CE, the great stone towers of Angkor had reached their peak. But empires, like the monsoon, have seasons. What rose with brilliance often settles back into the earth, and mainland Southeast Asia was about to reshuffle its map once again.

The Fall of the Great Builders (1250–1450 CE)

The Khmer Empire began to tire under its own weight. Its waterworks silted up, its nobles bickered, and its borders grew restless. New Thai kingdoms to the west—**Sukhothai**, then **Ayutthaya**—learned from the Khmer, borrowed their temple styles, and then quietly replaced them.

To the east, the **Cham** slipped into decline as **Dai Viet** (Vietnam) expanded southward, following its steady "March to the South". By the 1400s, the Khmer had lost much of their coast, and the great city of **Angkor Thom** was fading into the jungle. When the Siamese sacked it in 1431, the empire's long twilight began.

Kingdoms on the Move (1450–1800 CE)

Across the region, new capitals rose:

- **Ayutthaya** thrived on trade and diplomacy, playing China, India, and Europe off one another with brilliant diplomacy.
- The **Lan Xang** kingdom (in today's Laos) spread Buddhist monasteries instead of fortresses.

- The **Burmese** kings of **Pagan**, then **Ava**, then **Konbaung**, dreamed of uniting the Irrawaddy Valley—and occasionally succeeded.
- In **Vietnam**, the Trinh and Nguyen families quarrelled endlessly while still expanding rice fields southward toward the Mekong.

Europe was arriving, too—first the **Portuguese** and **Dutch**, then the **French** and **British**—drawn by spices, silk, and opportunity. For centuries, Mainland Southeast Asia had been shaped by India and China; now the West added a third weight to the scale.

The Colonial Patchwork (1800–1945 CE)

By the nineteenth century, the map looked like a colonial jigsaw.

Burma became British.

Vietnam, **Laos**, and **Cambodia** became French Indochina.

Thailand (Siam) alone kept its independence—by trading and signing beneficial treaties.

The colonial governments built railways, schools, and grand administrative buildings—but also drew borders with little regard for culture or tribe. Resistance simmered. When the Japanese swept through during World War II, they broke Europe's spell. When they retreated, independence movements were already marching.

Freedom and Friction (1945–1990 CE)

The post-war decades were noisy.

Vietnam fought first the French, then the Americans, finally reunifying in 1975. **Cambodia** fell under the **Khmer Rouge** (1975–79), whose rule brought horror instead of glory. **Laos** turned communist but quietly. **Thailand** juggled coups, kings, and capitalism, somehow keeping all three. **Myanmar** (Burma) shut its doors under military rule.

It was an era of ideology and rebuilding, when rice yields mattered more than relics and old temples waited patiently beneath the trees.

Opening Doors (1990–2025 CE)

With the Cold War over, the region re-opened to the world. Tourism poured in; significant efforts to clear **Angkor Wat** and **Bayon** resumed from 1985. They astonished visitors once again. **Luang Prabang** charmed, **Bagan** rose from its dust, and **Vietnam's** cities hummed with motorbikes and ambition.

The **ASEAN** group of nations—sometimes more family than club—worked to keep the peace while competing for trade.

By 2025, mainland Southeast Asia had returned to what it had always been: a place of resilience and reinvention, where people keep faith, trade stories, and rebuild after every storm.

The temples of **Angkor** and **Bayon** still stand, silent witnesses to 800 years of drama—from kings and conquerors to tourists with cameras—proving that in Southeast Asia, even chaos has a kind of continuity.

About the author

Gavin P. Fraser was born in George, South Africa, in 1958. He graduated in Chemical Engineering from the University of Cape Town and began his career in the oil industry, working by day and singing opera by night while completing both an MBA and a degree in Musicology.

A move to London in the early 1990s brought him into the world of international management consulting. Over the next two decades he worked in more than 35 countries, specialising in organisation transformation, business strategy, innovation, leadership development and corporate culture change.

Gavin's fascination with sacred spaces began at the age of thirteen, when his parents took him to a Hindu temple in Durban, South Africa. The colours, statues and incense made a lifelong impression. Since then, he has visited several hundred temples, shrines and sacred sites across Southern, South-Eastern and Eastern Asia. These include Buddhist (both Theravada and Mahayana), Hindu, Jain, Sikh, Shinto and Daoist traditions.

Whether wandering through the vast corridors of the Sri Arulmigu Ramanathaswamy Temple in Rameswaram, exploring the ruins of My Son in Vietnam, sitting quietly in the garden of a Kyoto shrine, or climbing a hillside in Taiwan to visit its famous Daoist temples, these places have shaped his curiosity about history, art, religion and the human need to create meaning in stone.

Alongside his business life, Gavin recorded two albums of original songs and recorded Mozart's Symphonies Nos. 40 and 41 with the Danube Symphony Orchestra—recordings that went on to become among the most streamed interpretations of these classics worldwide.

He now divides his time between writing books and music, designing gardens, and travelling widely. His books include *The Nine Values That Shaped Great Britain: Why "Nice" Won't Save Us*, *The Moral Stress of Nations*, *Angkor & Bayon: Unveiling the Meaning and Mysteries*, and *Why We Hate Each Other*.

He is based between the UK, Europe, and Asia, and has three children.